PATTERNS OF PEACE
MANDALAS FOR MINDFUL COLORING

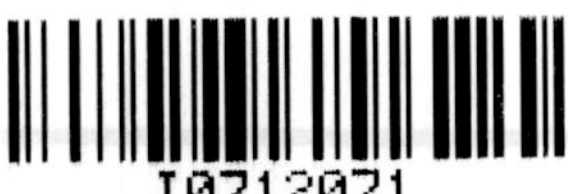

THIS COLORING BOOK
BELONGS TO

COLOR TEST PAGE

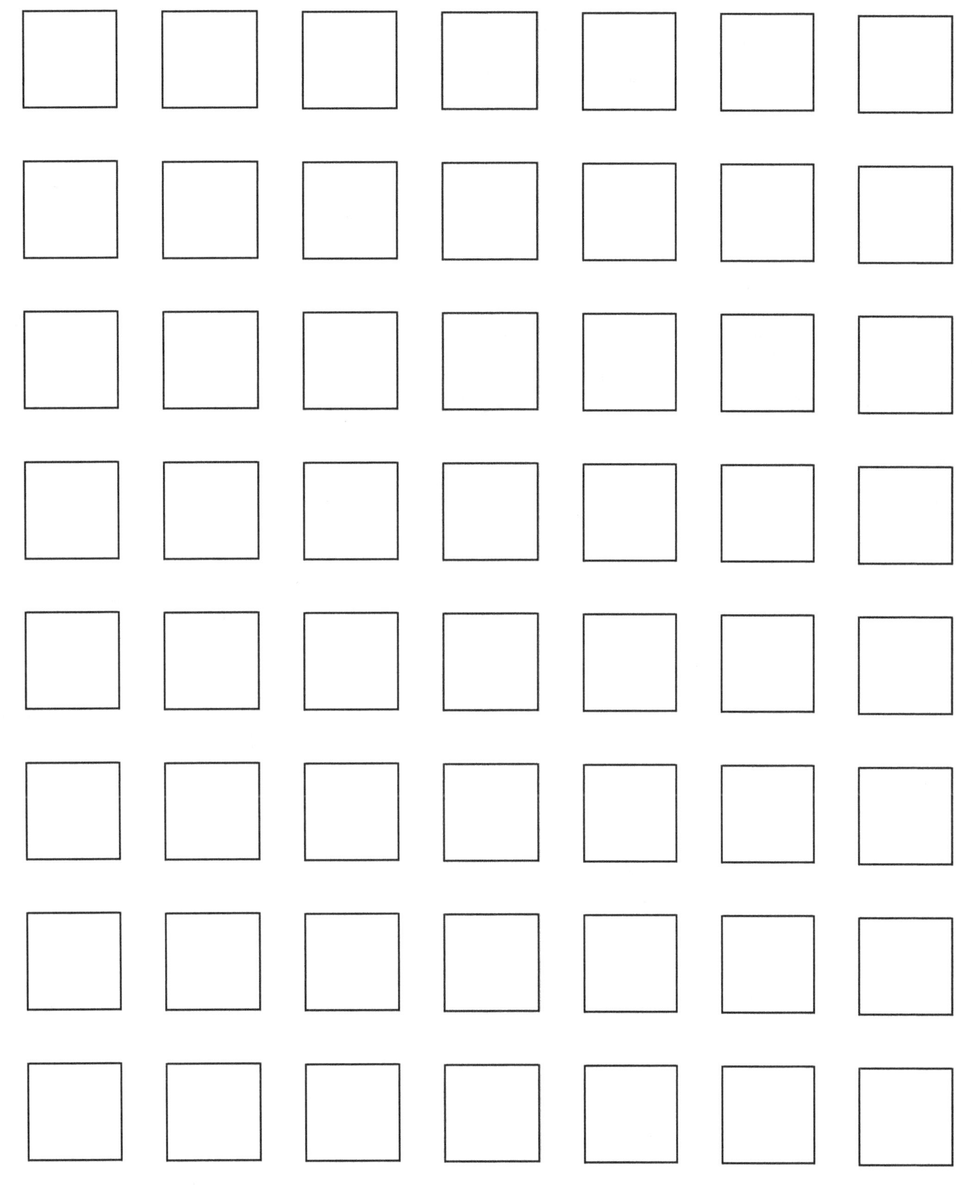

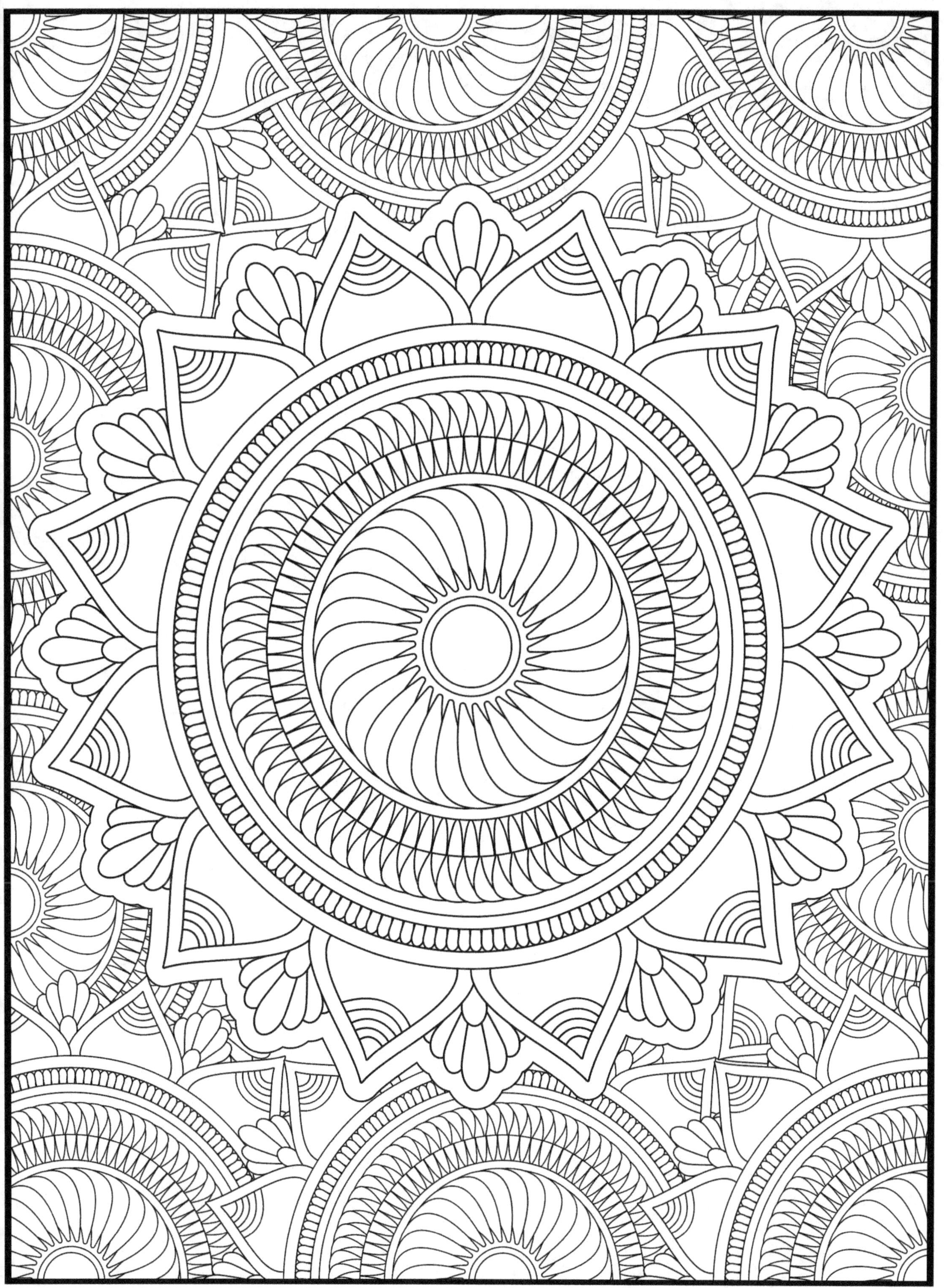

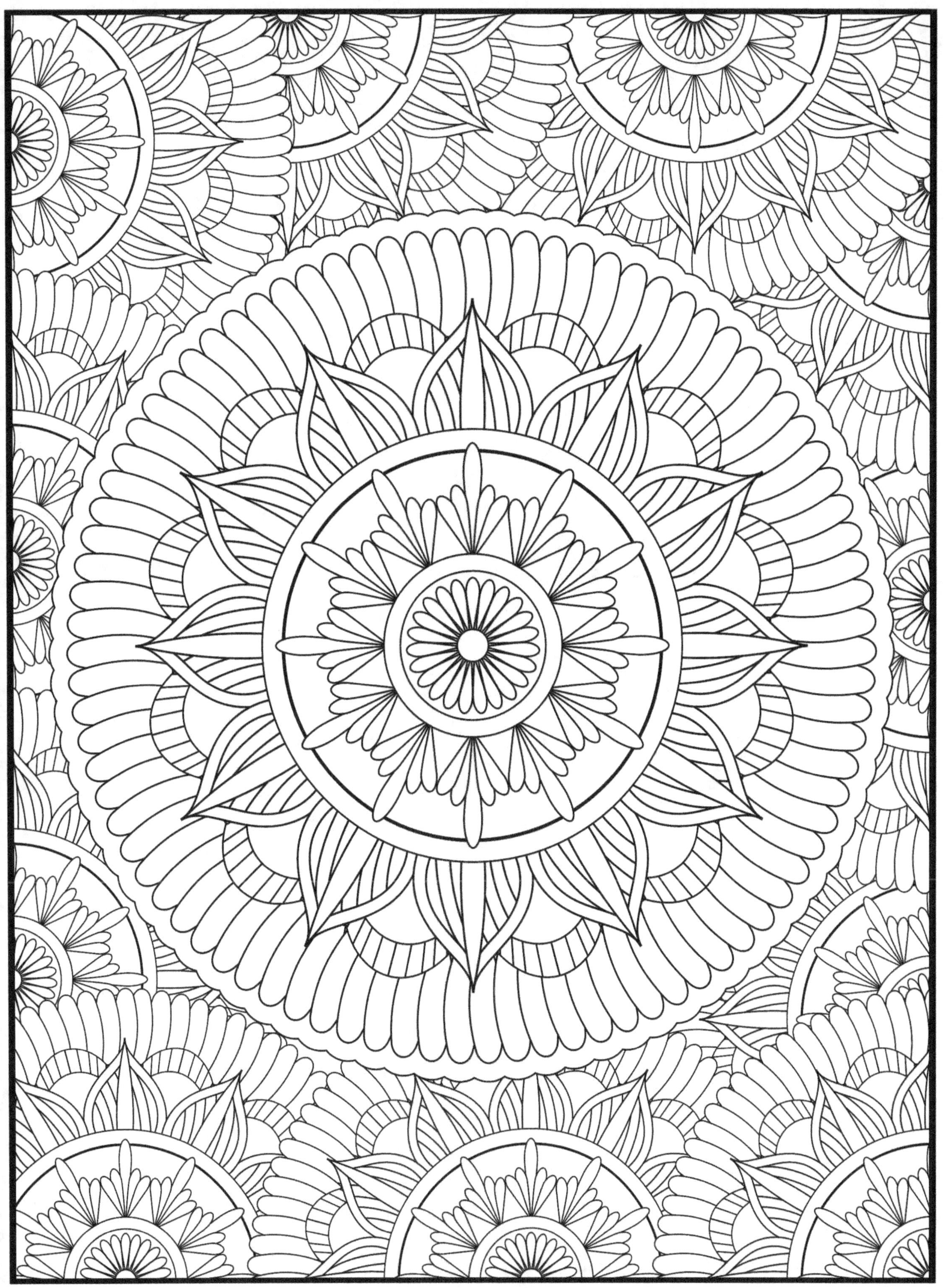

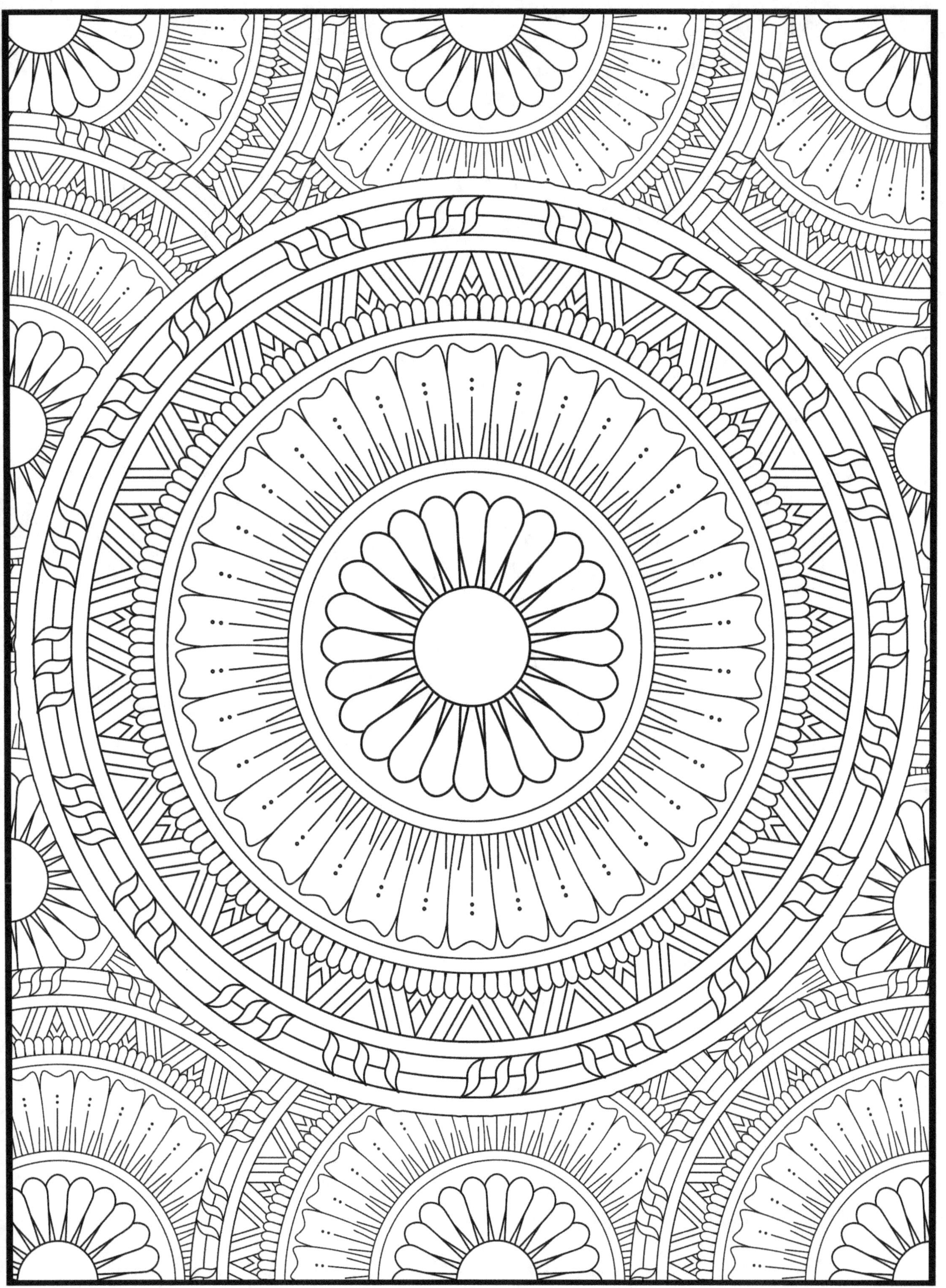

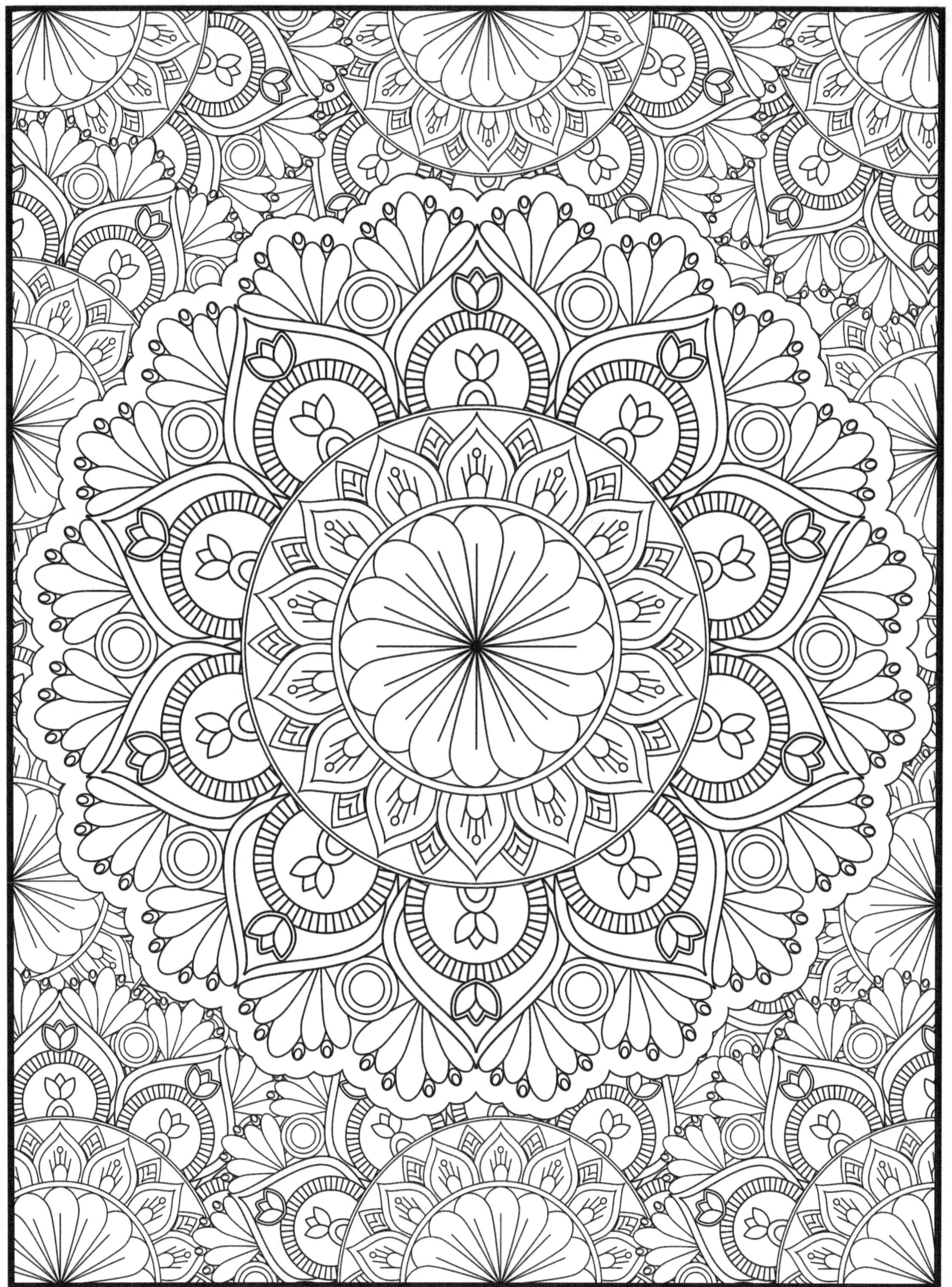

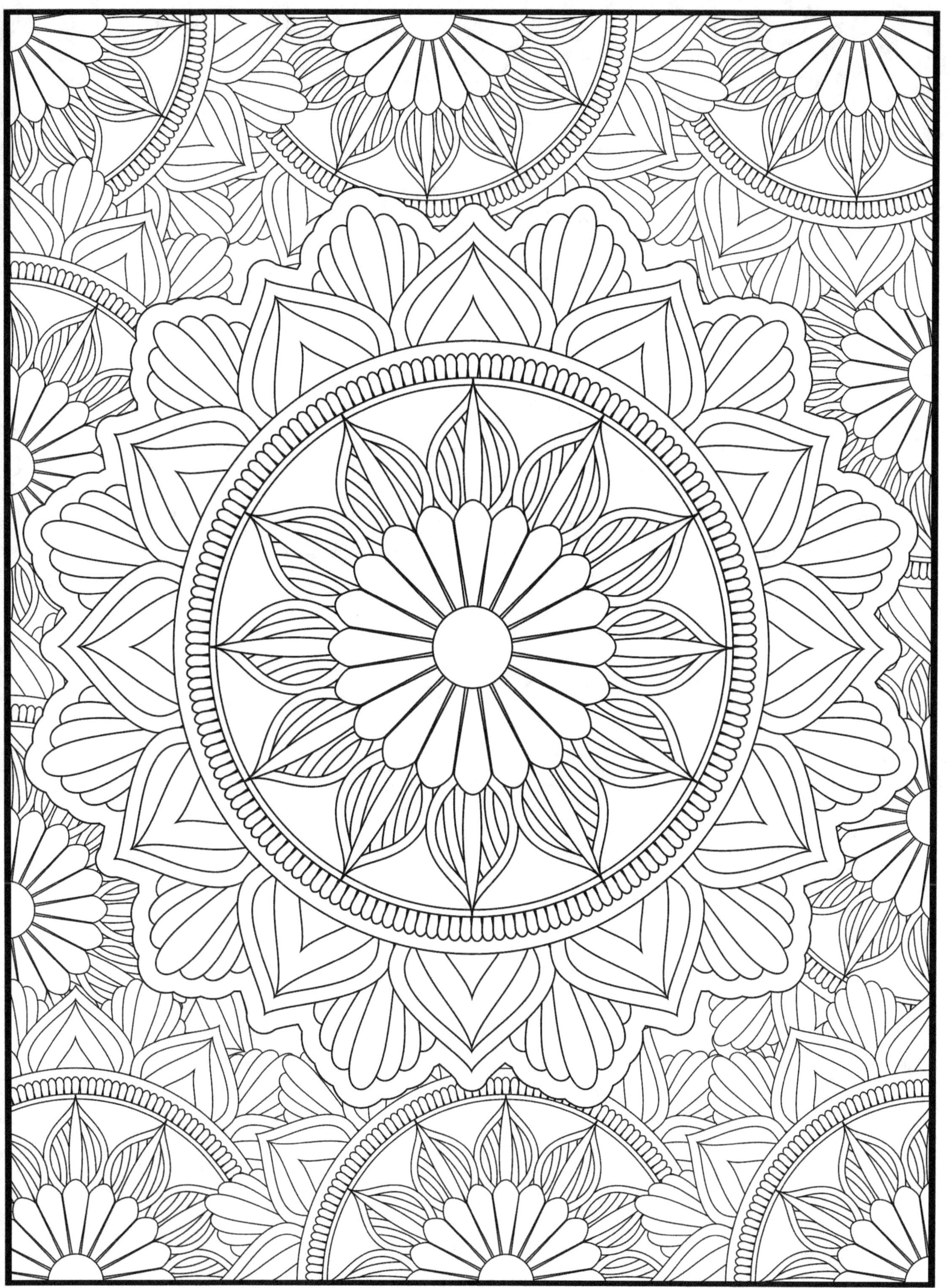

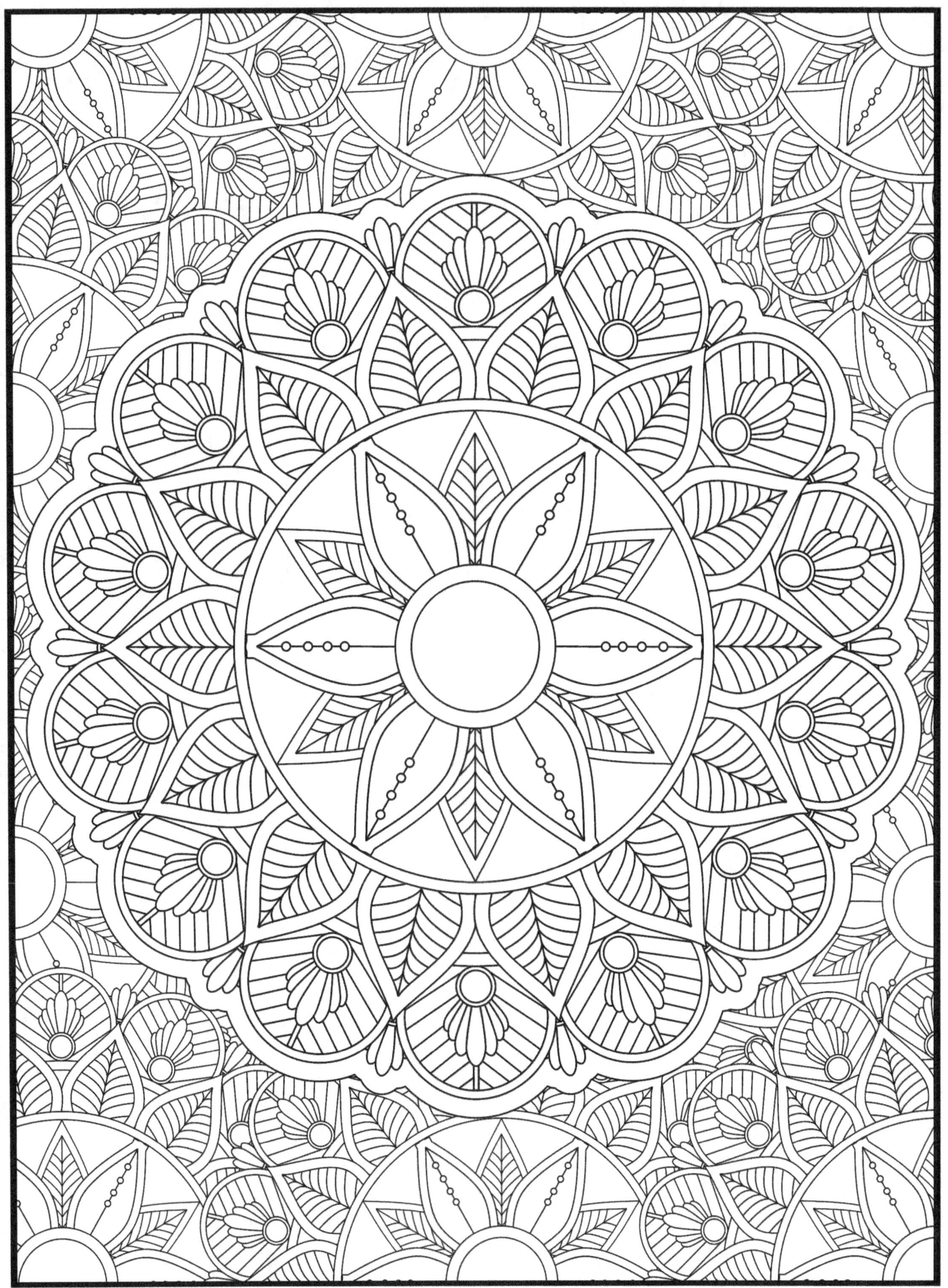

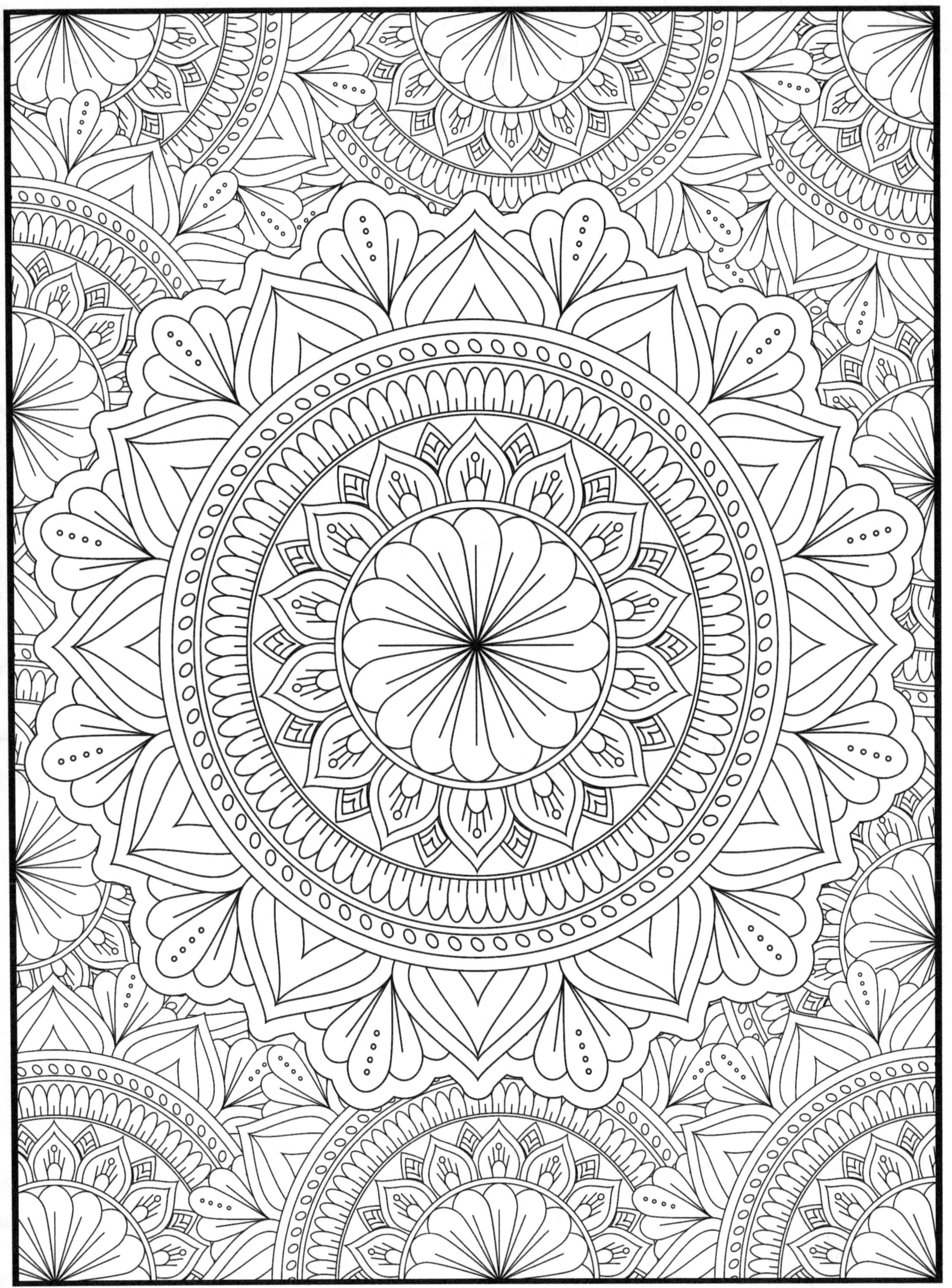

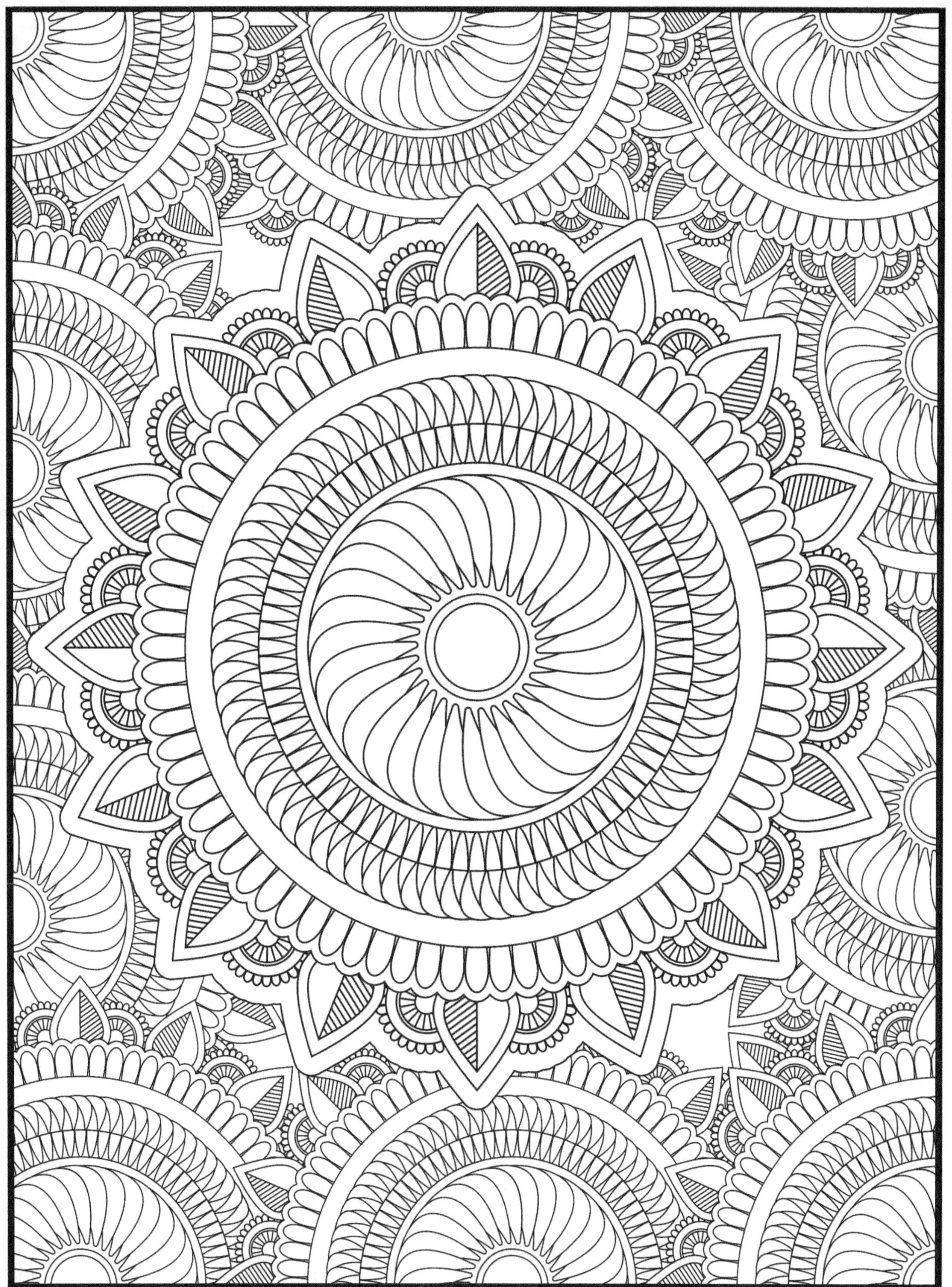

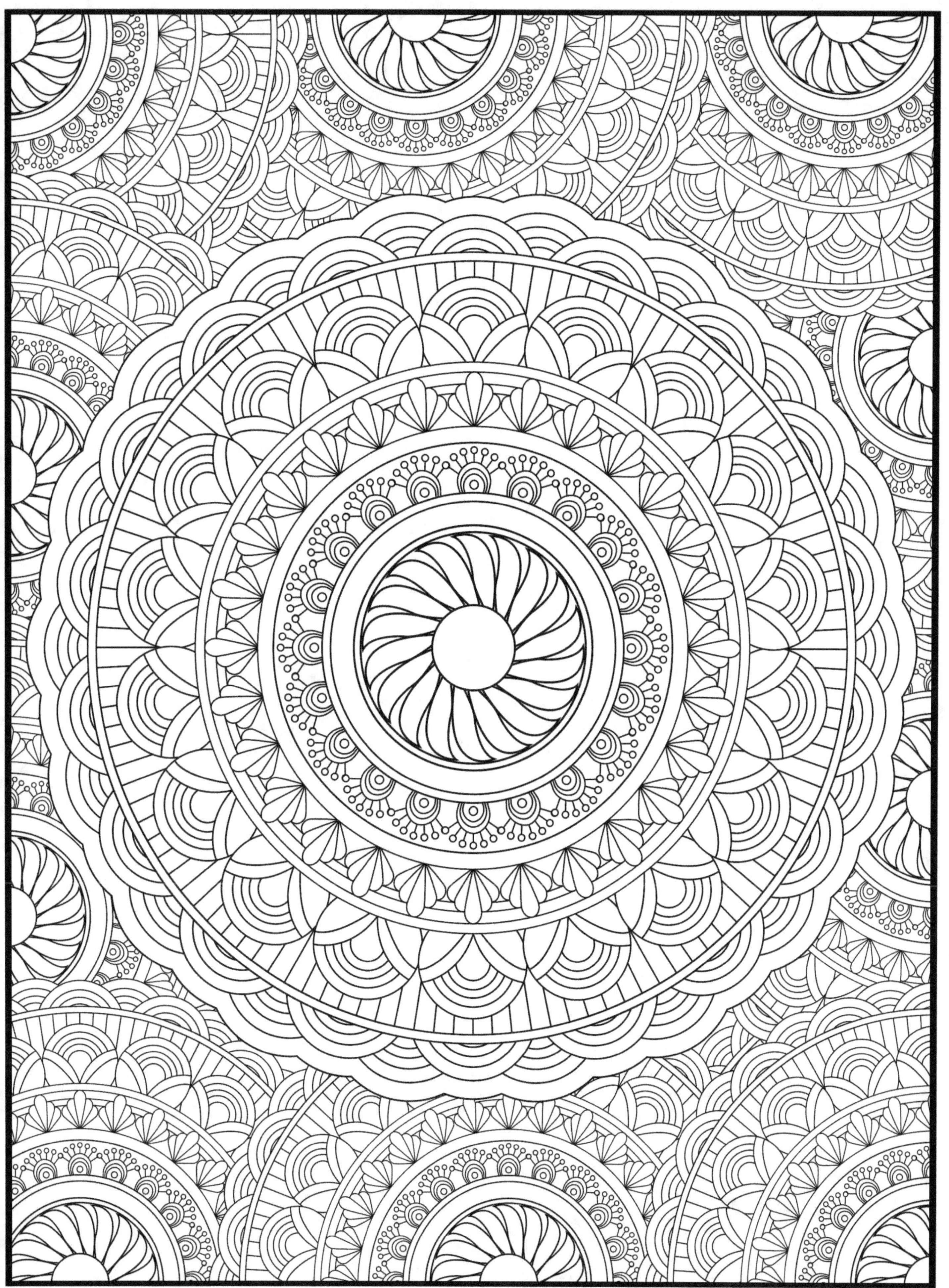

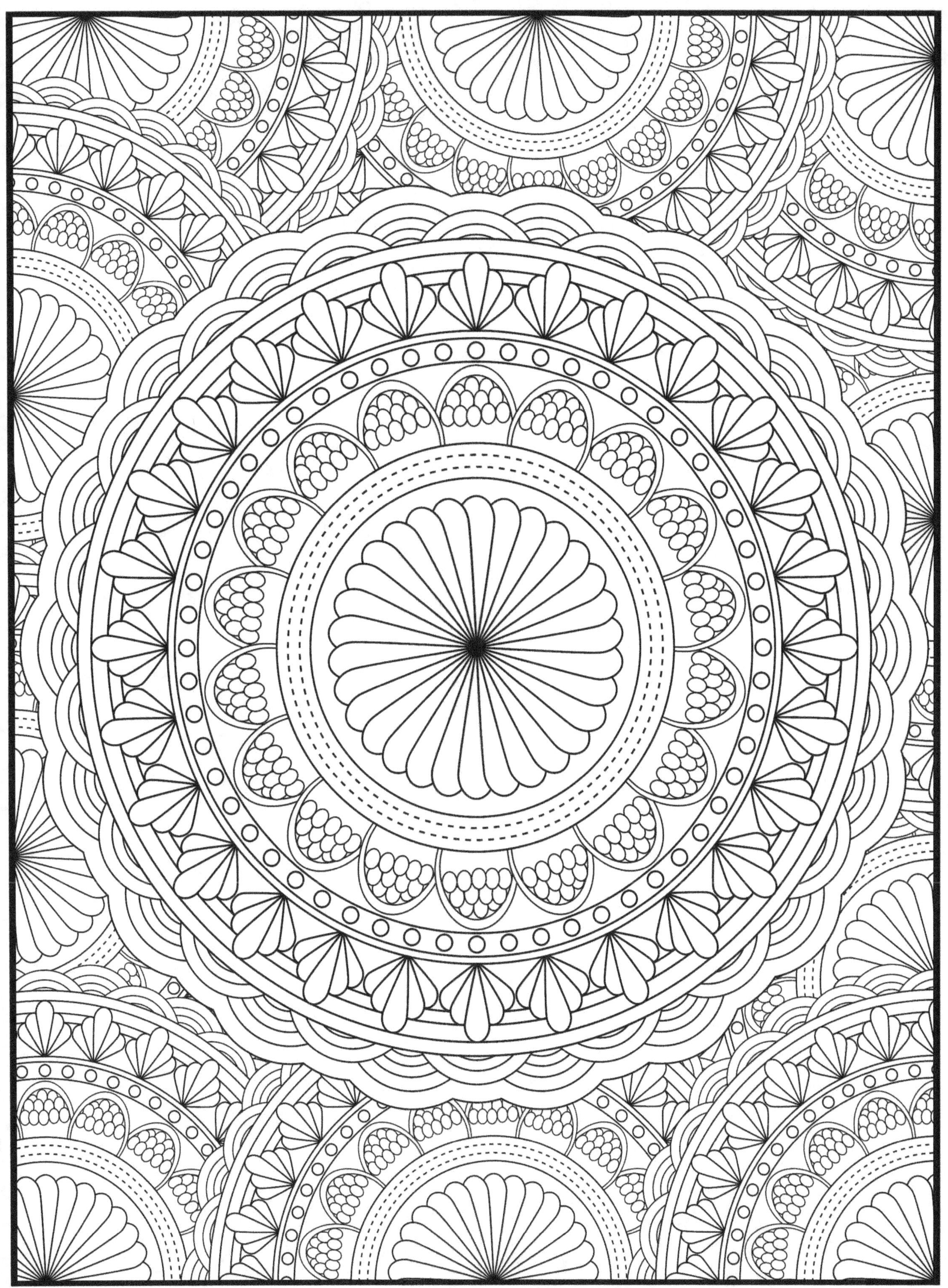

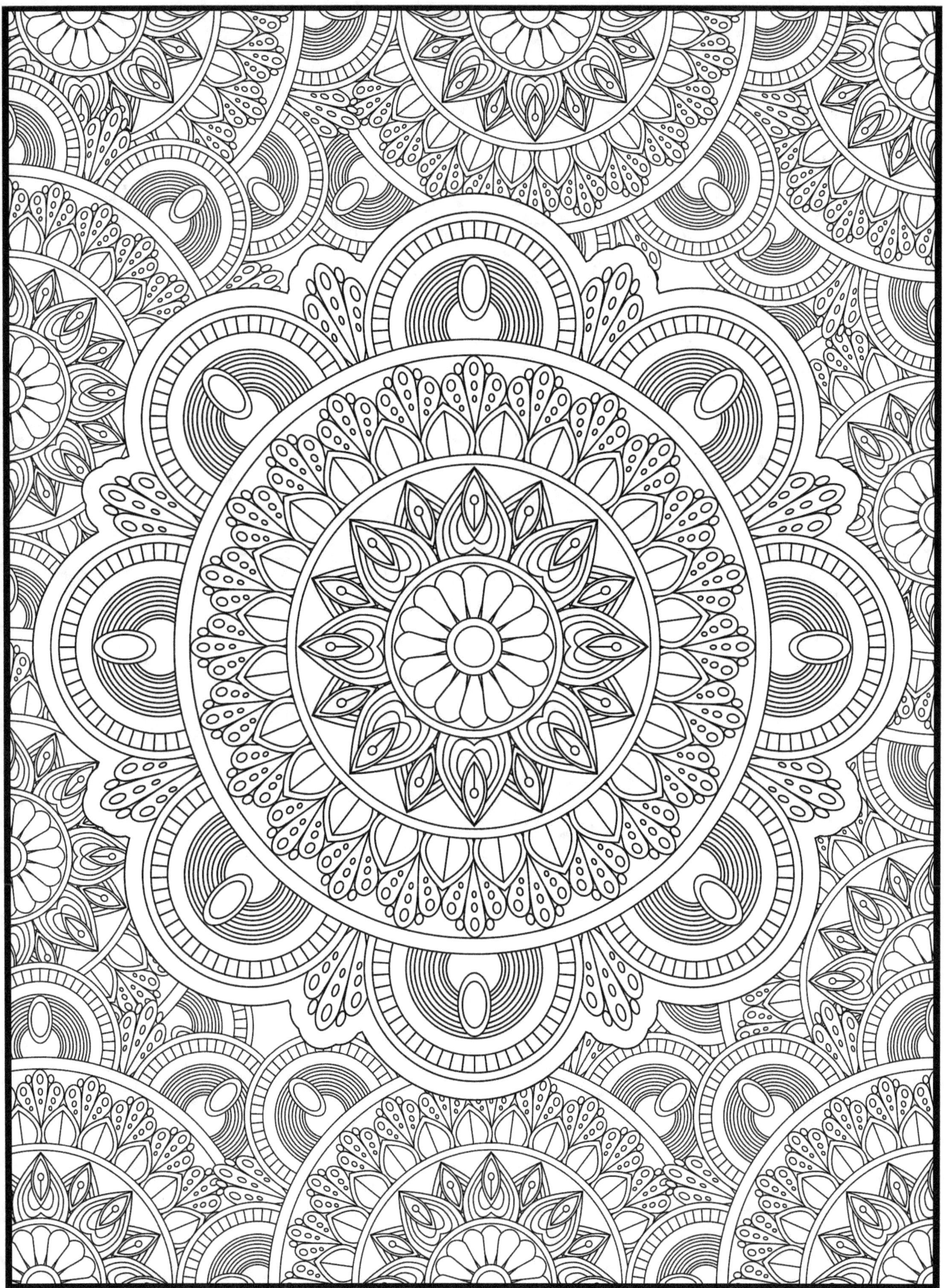

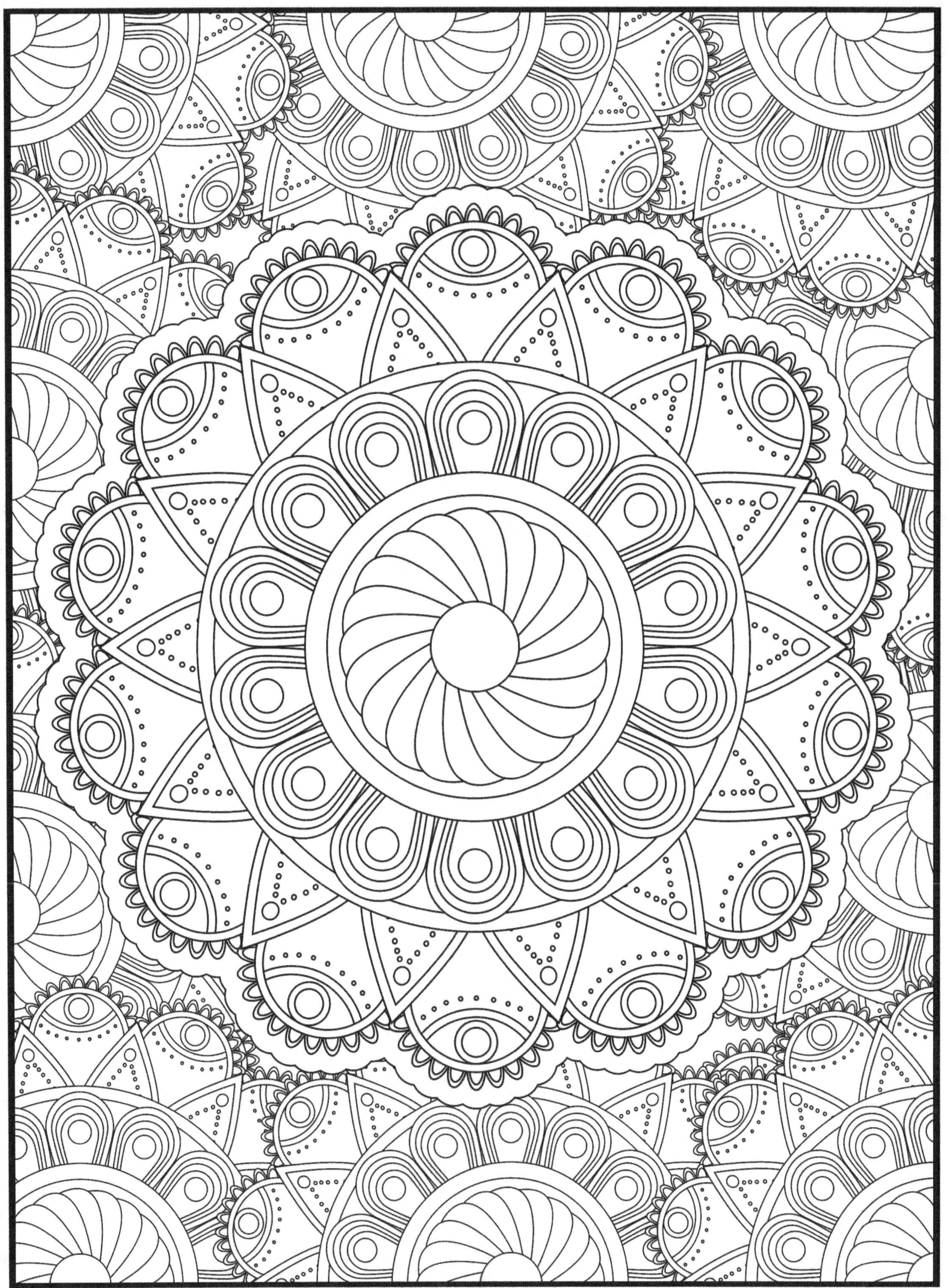

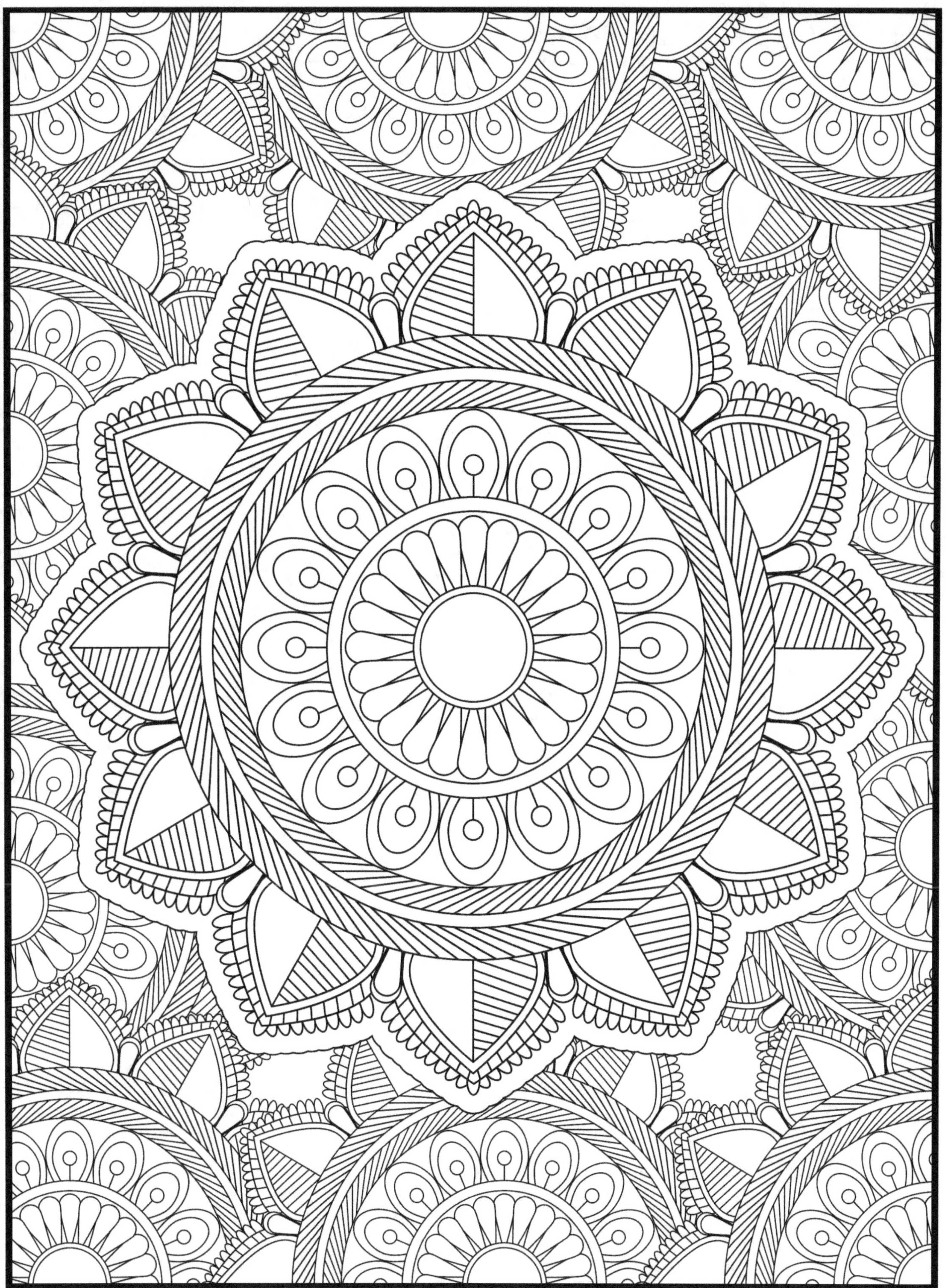

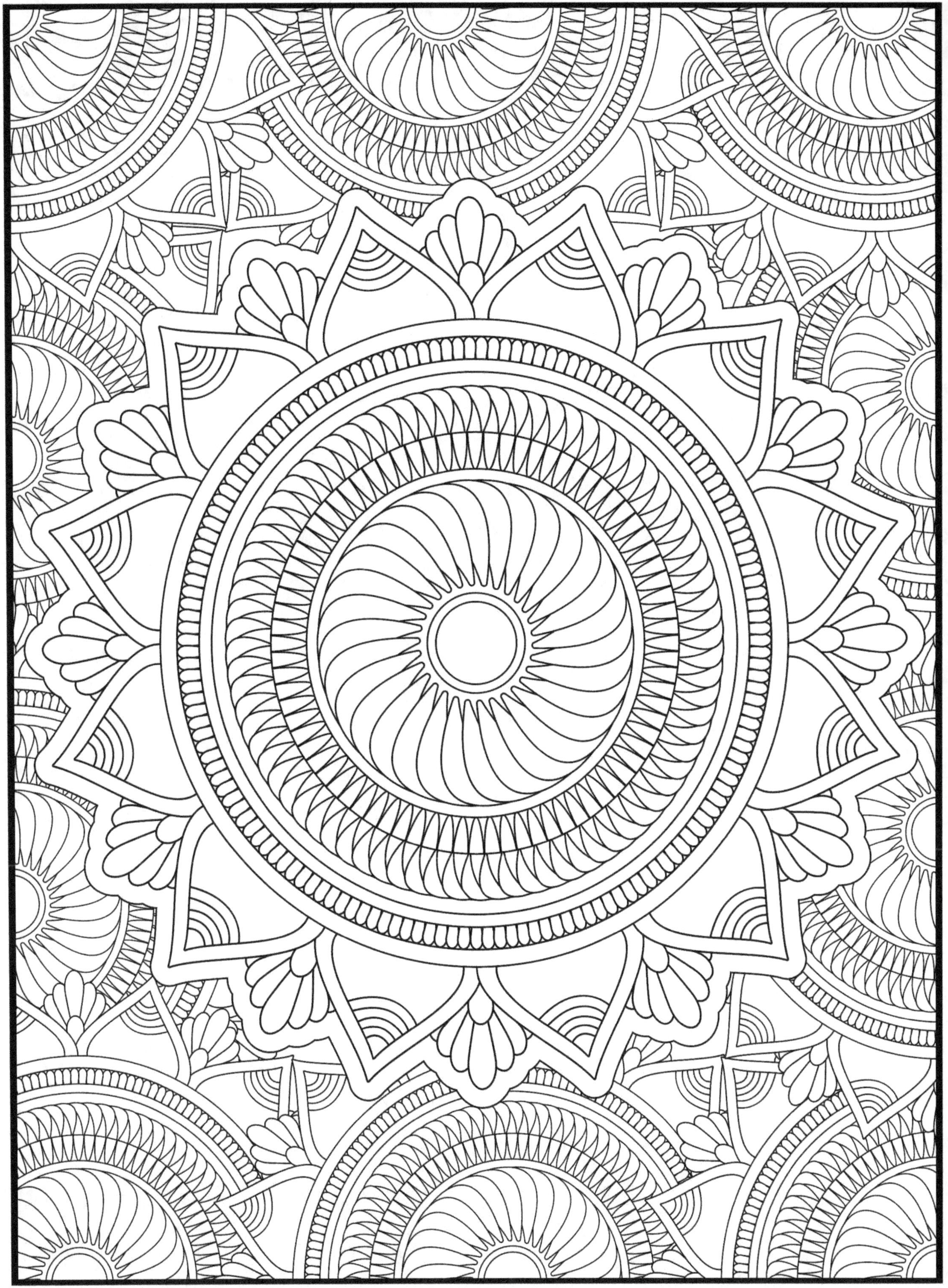

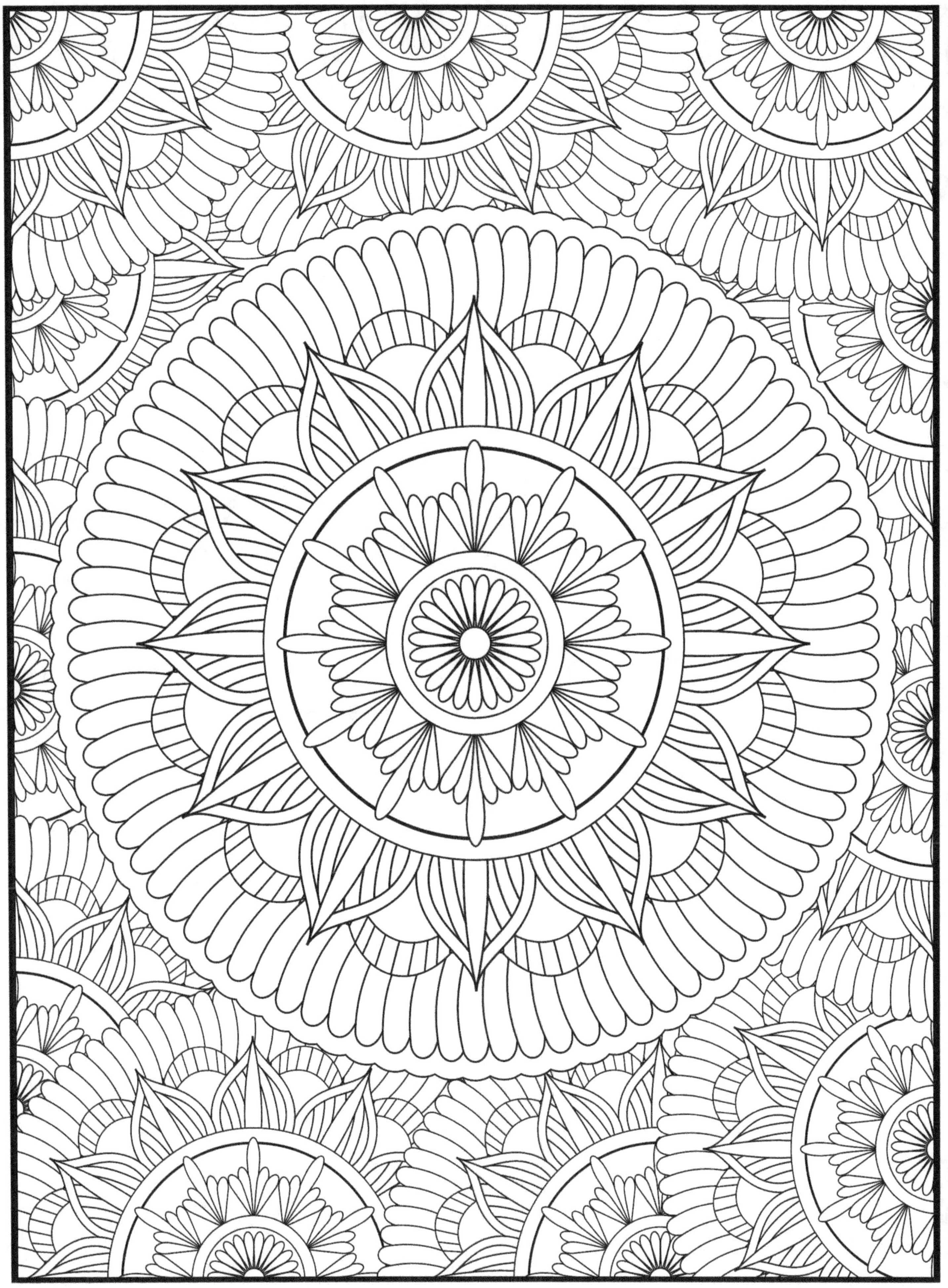

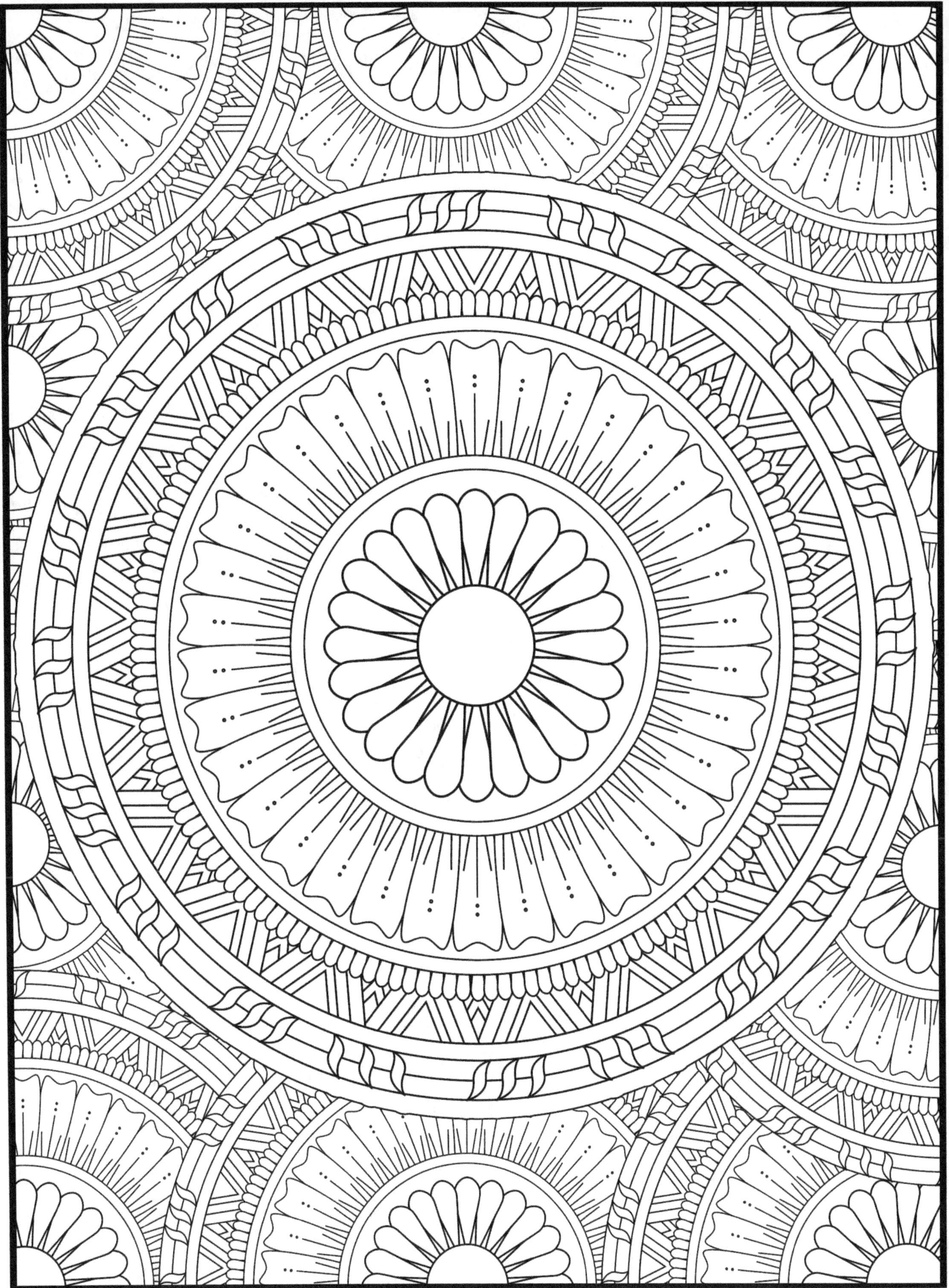

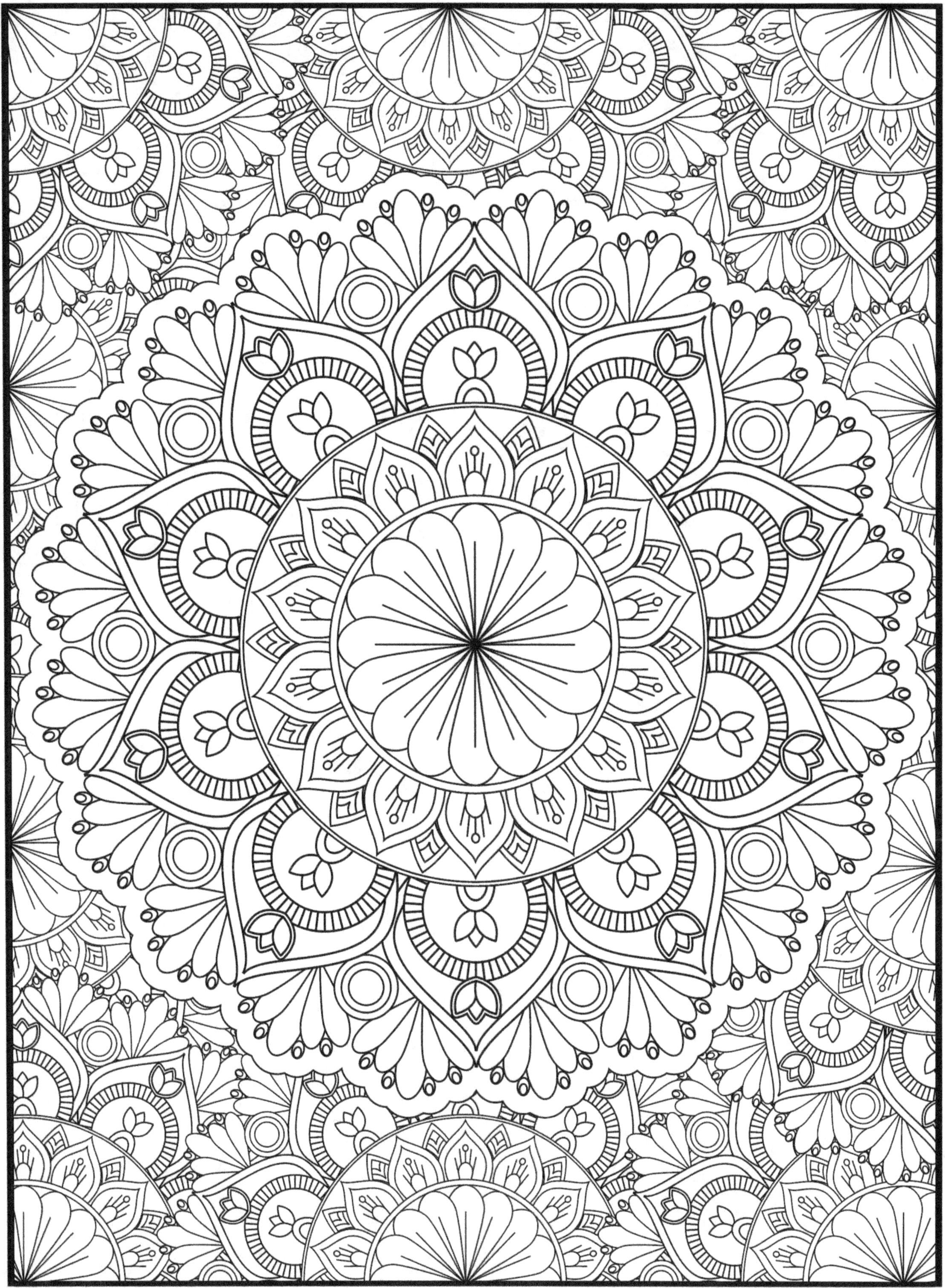

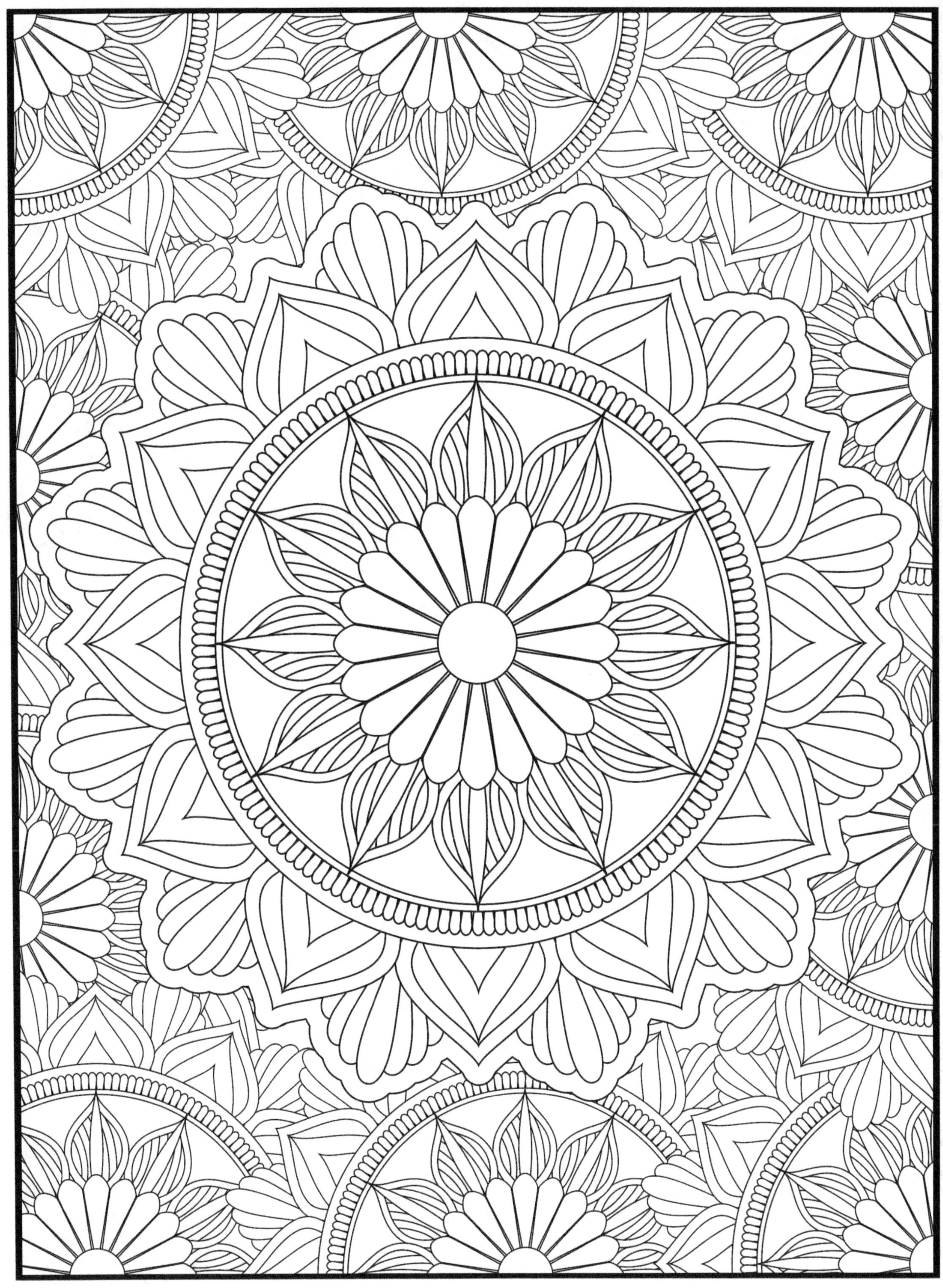

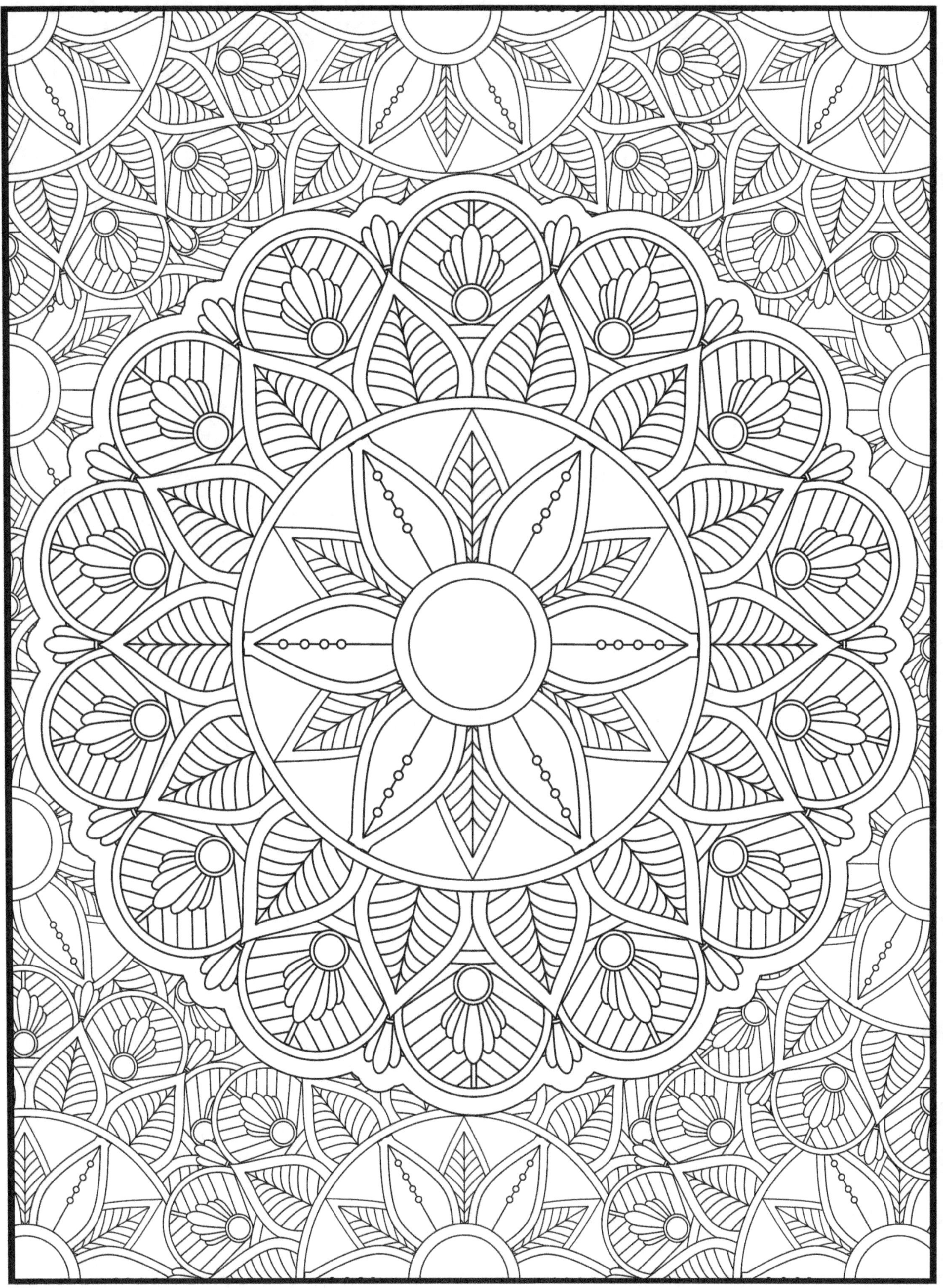

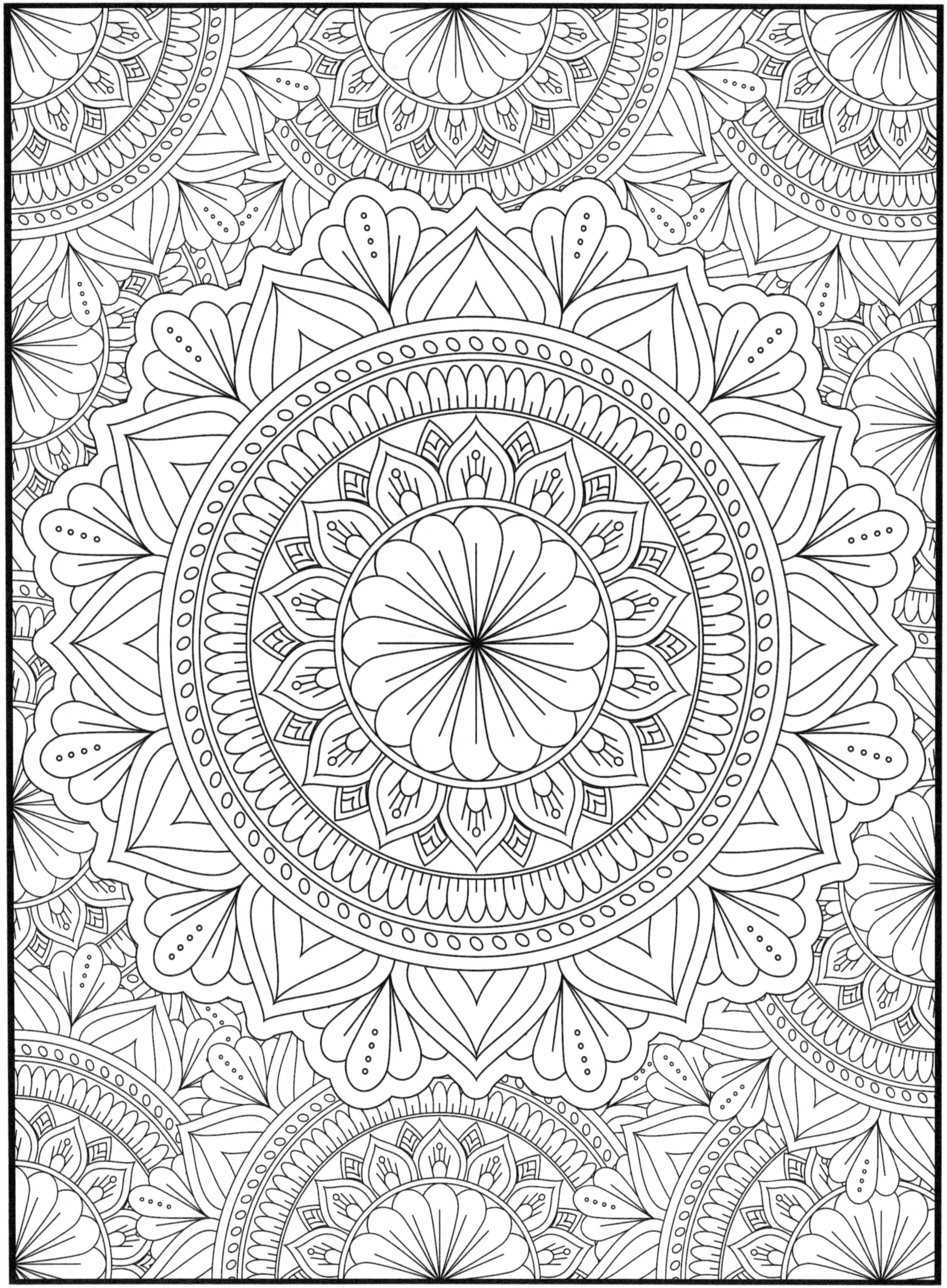

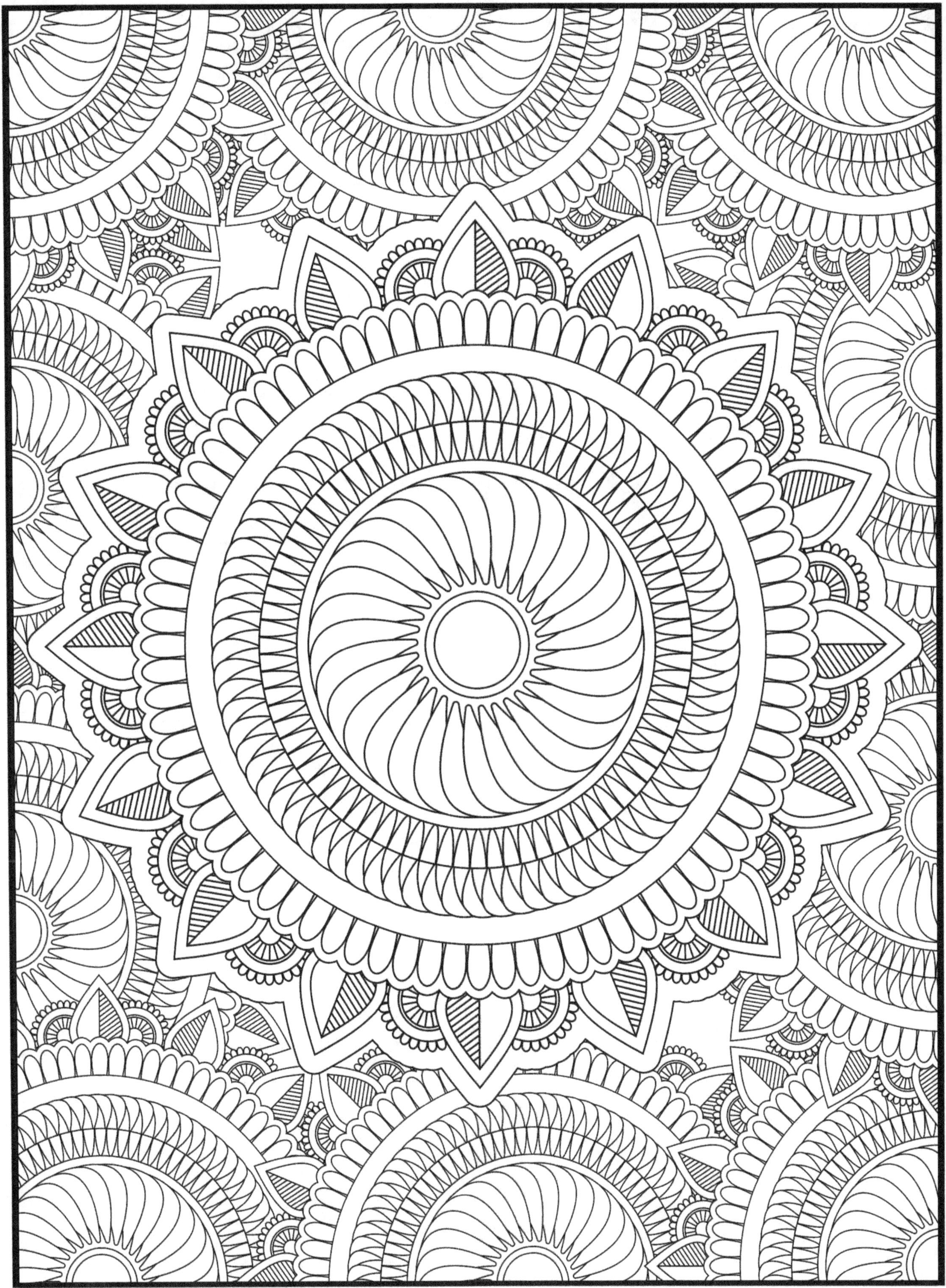

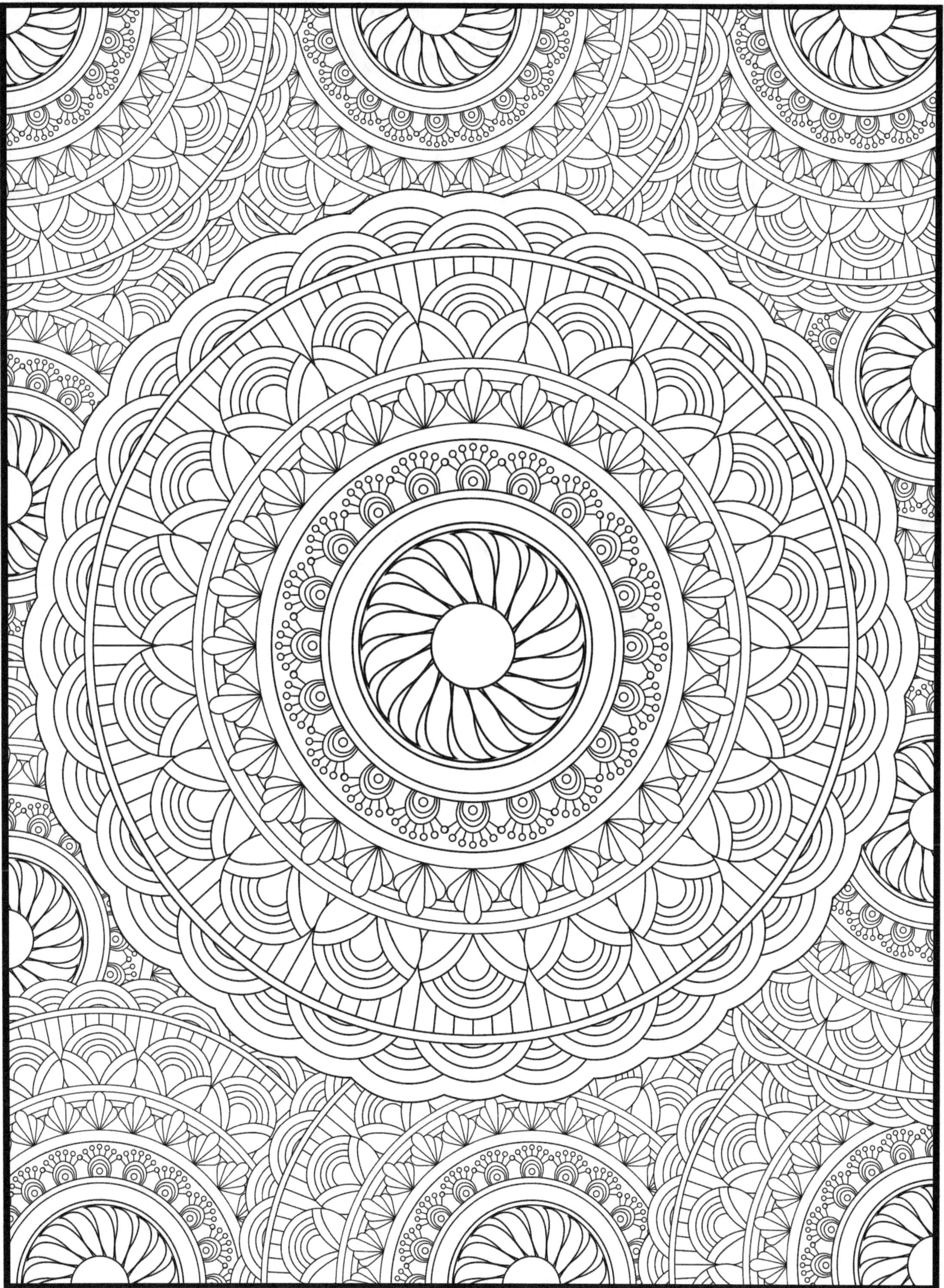

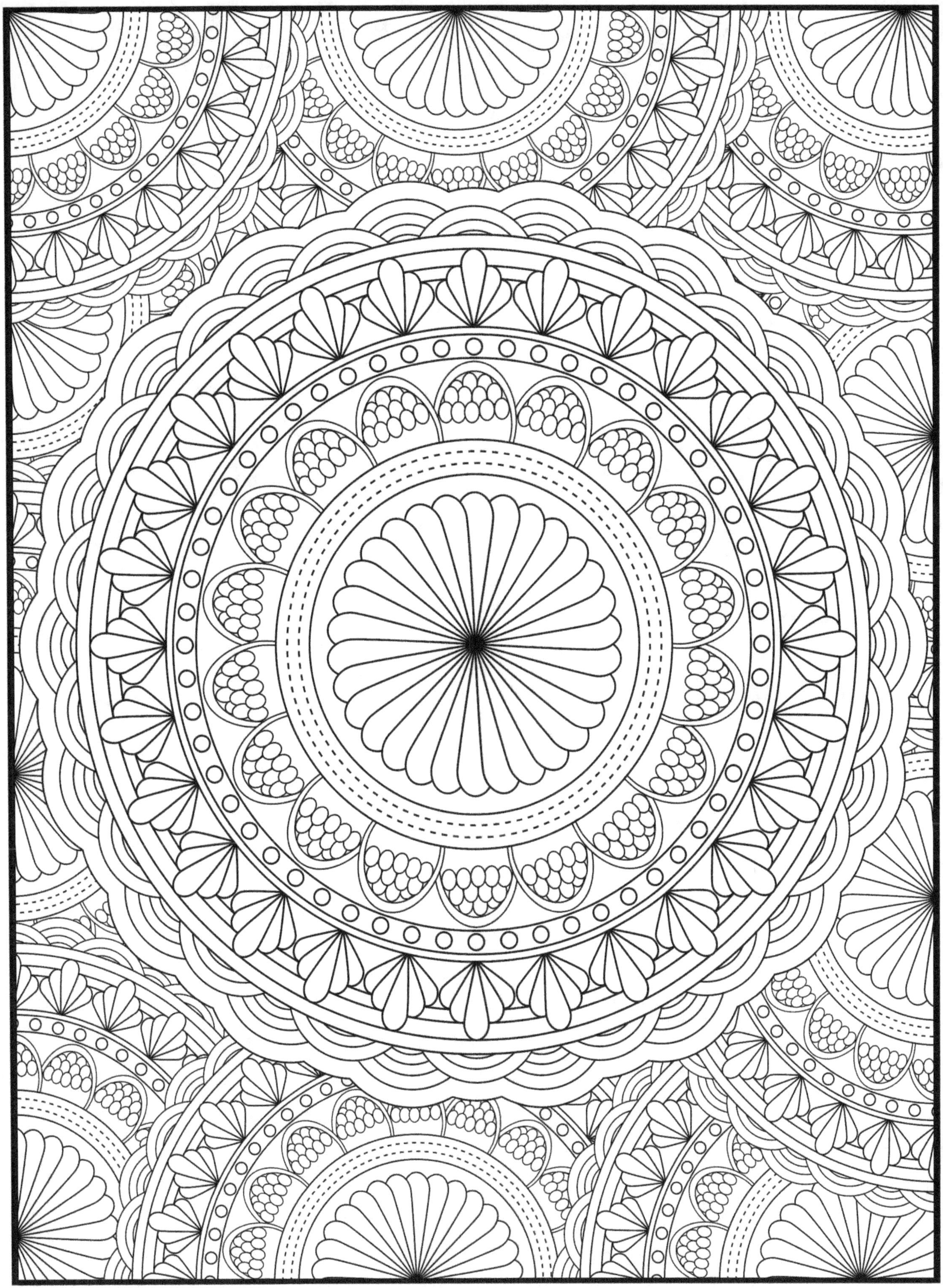

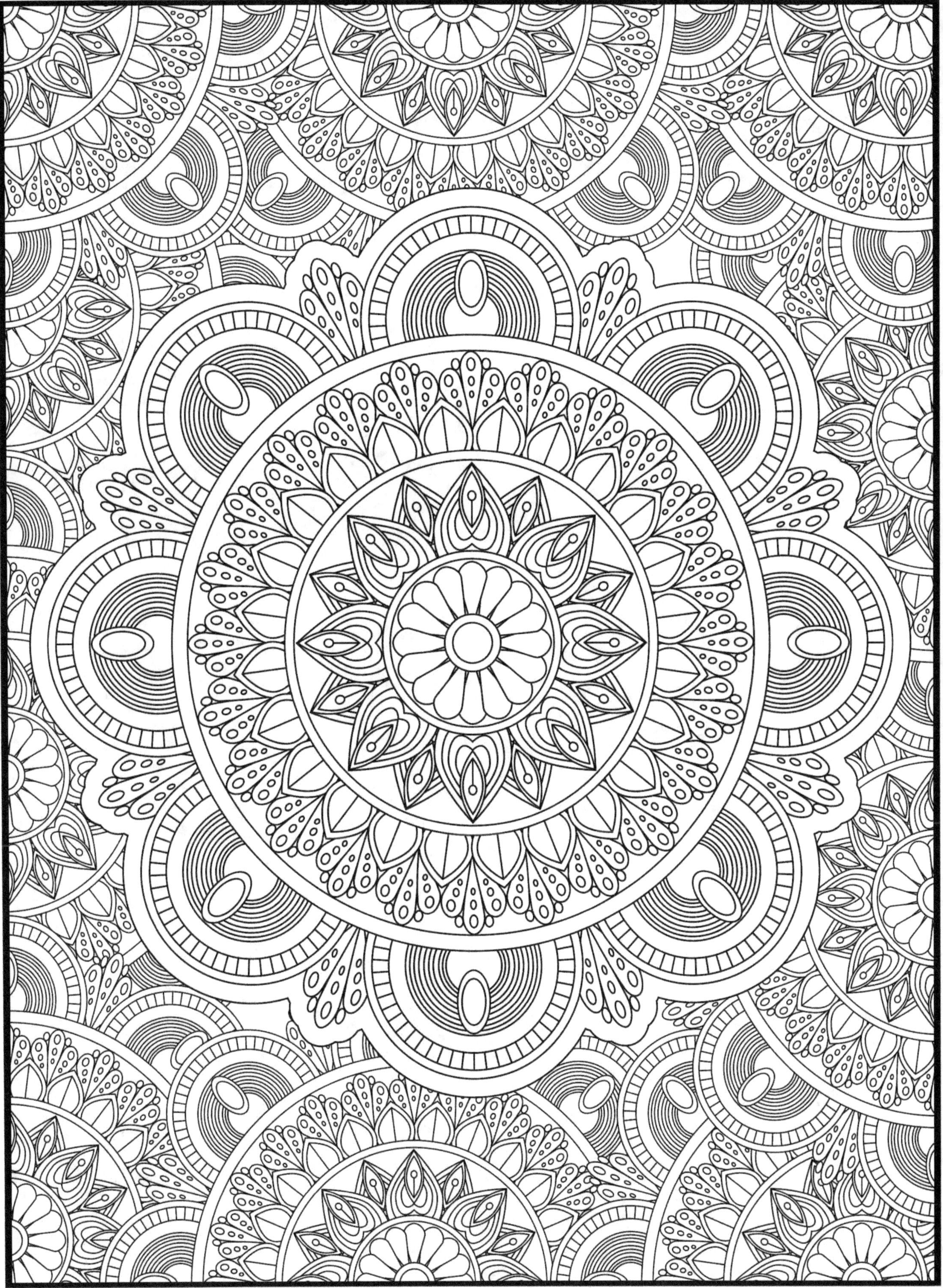

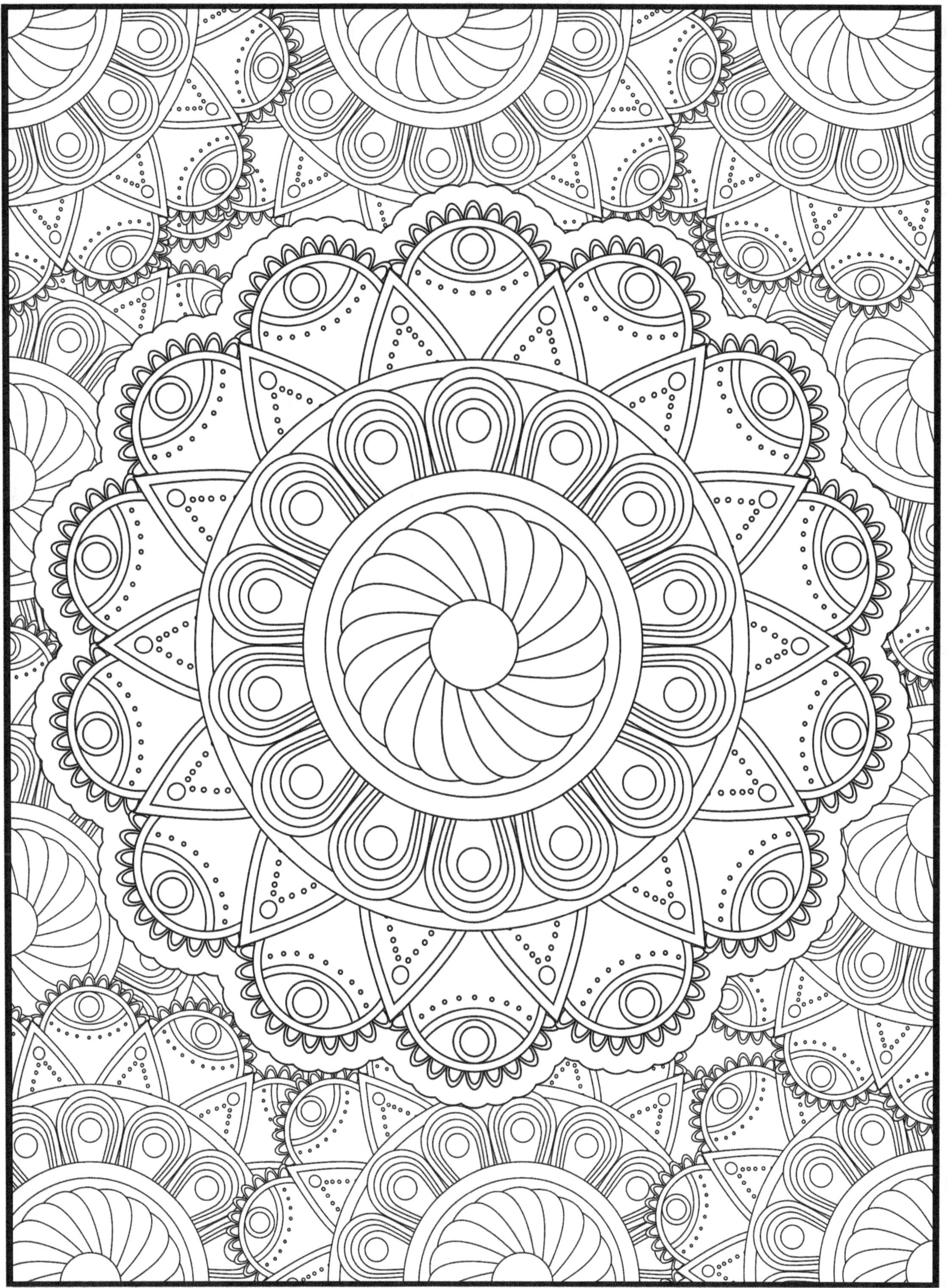

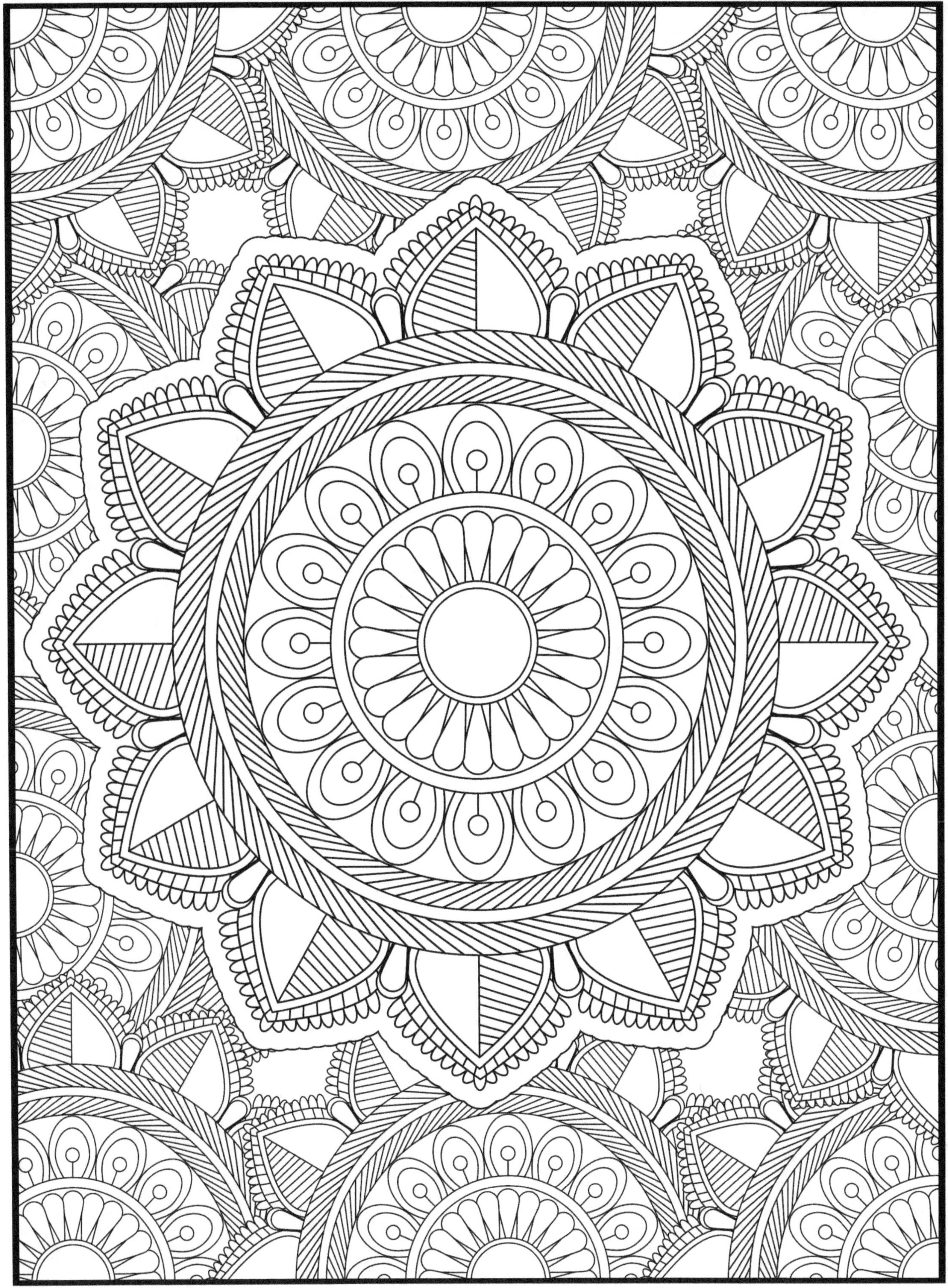

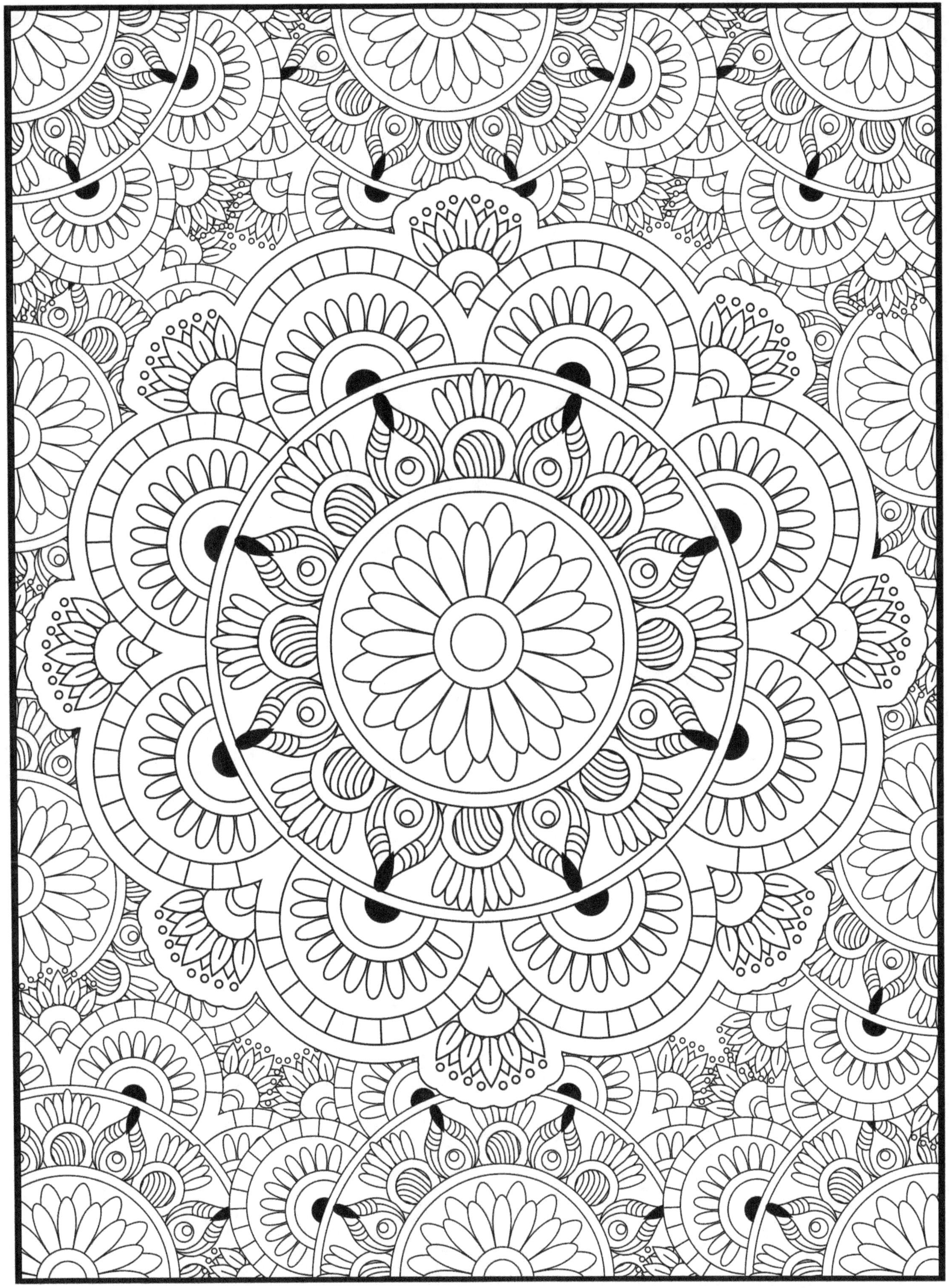

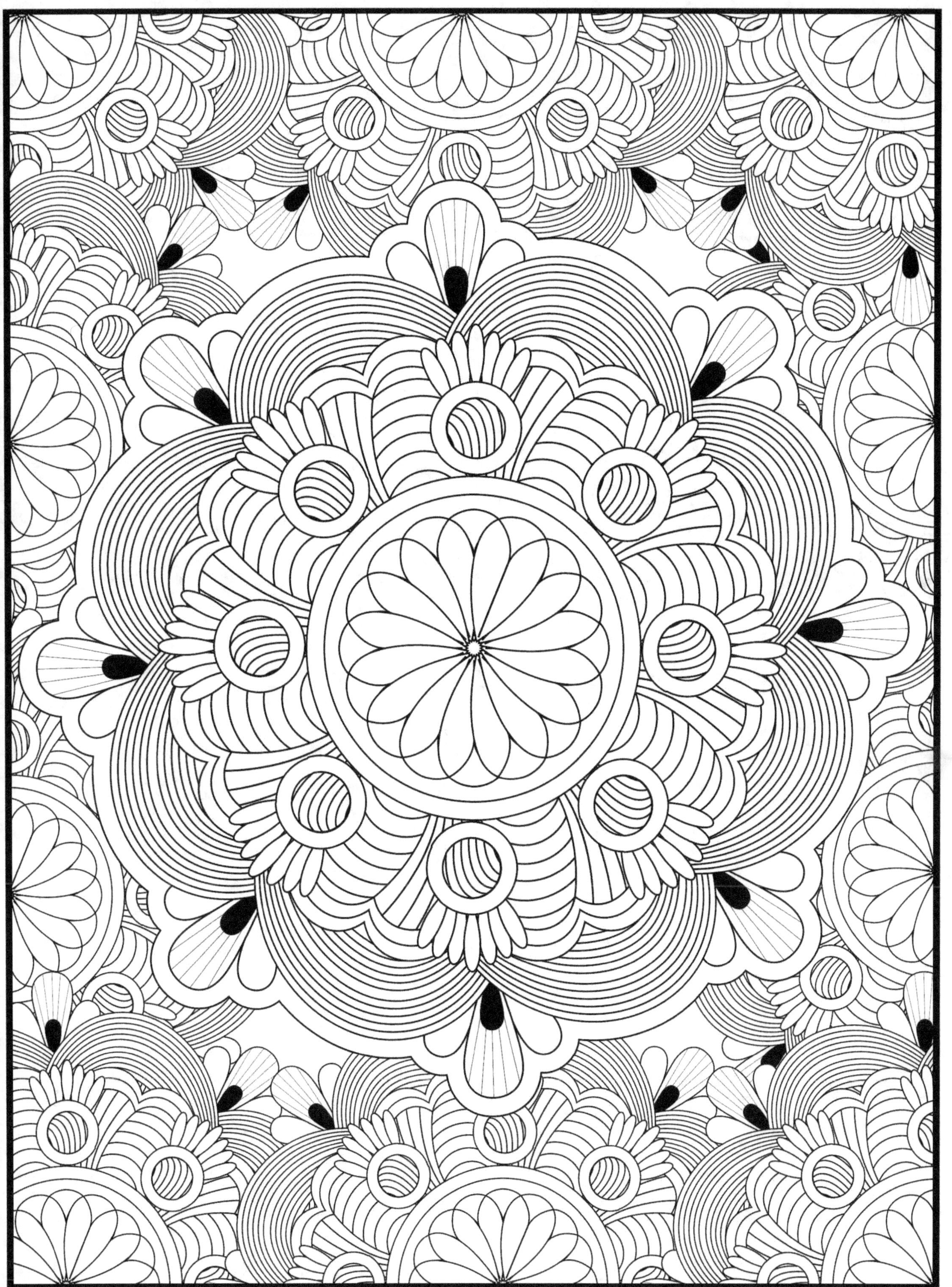

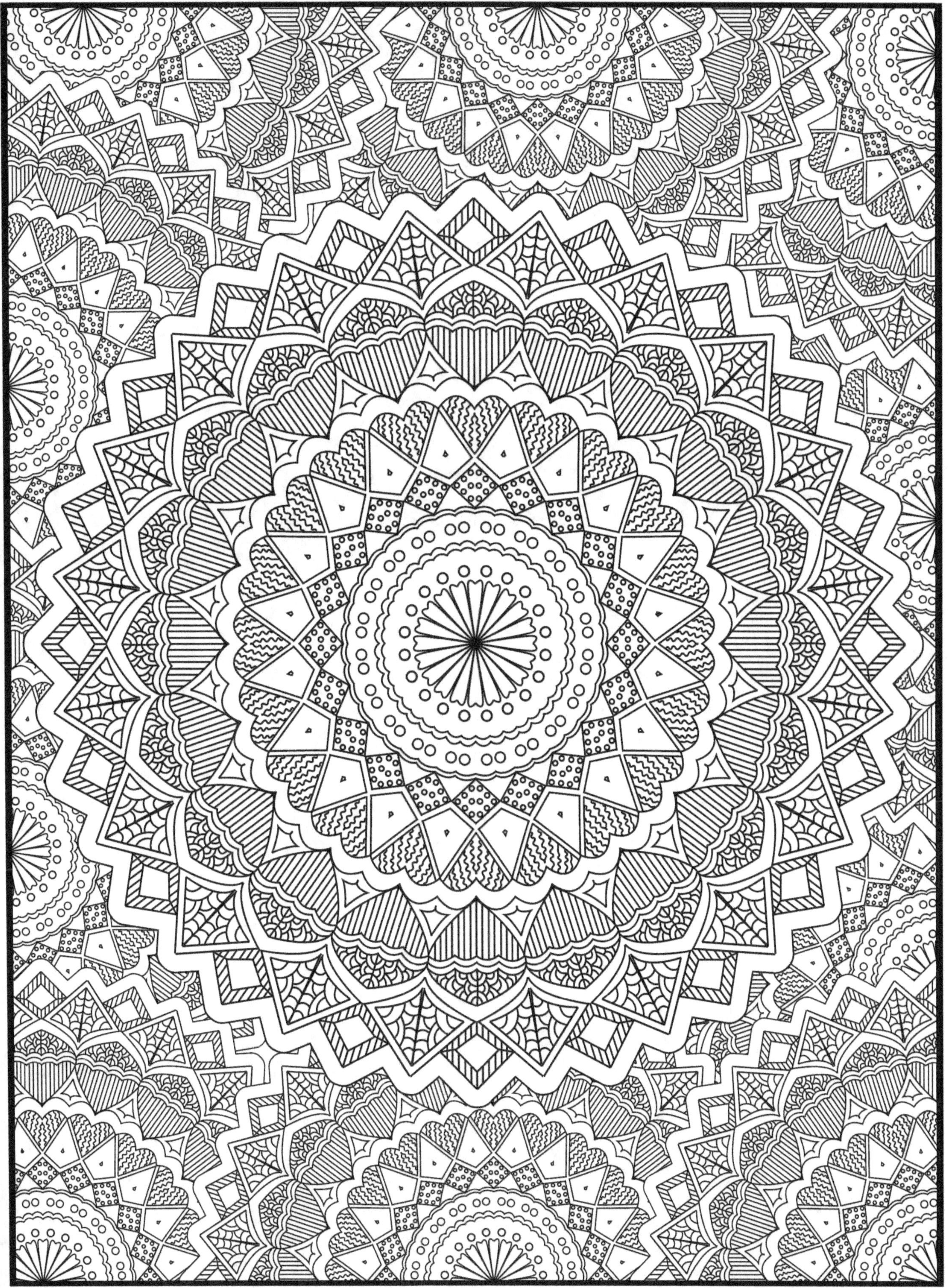

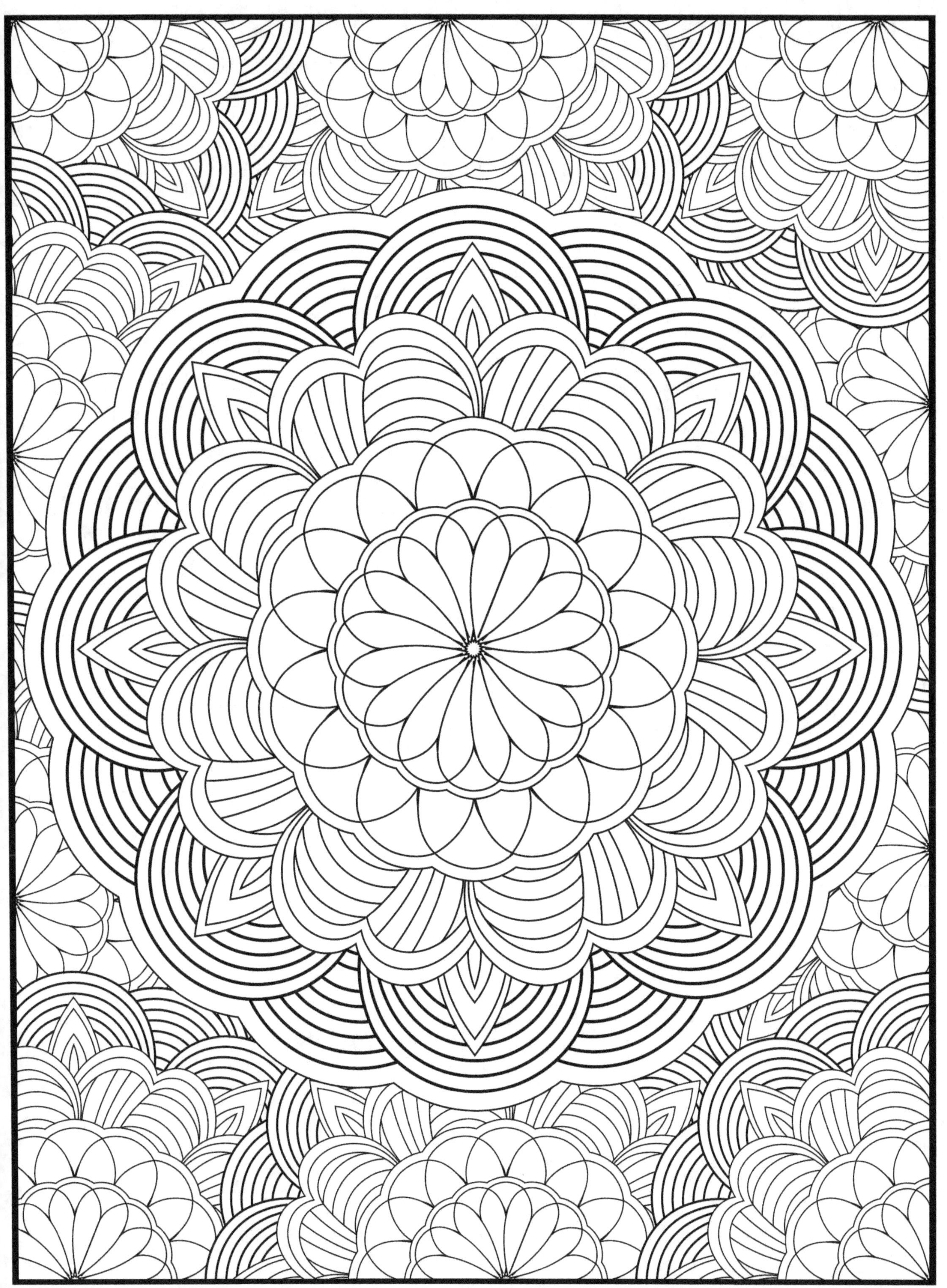

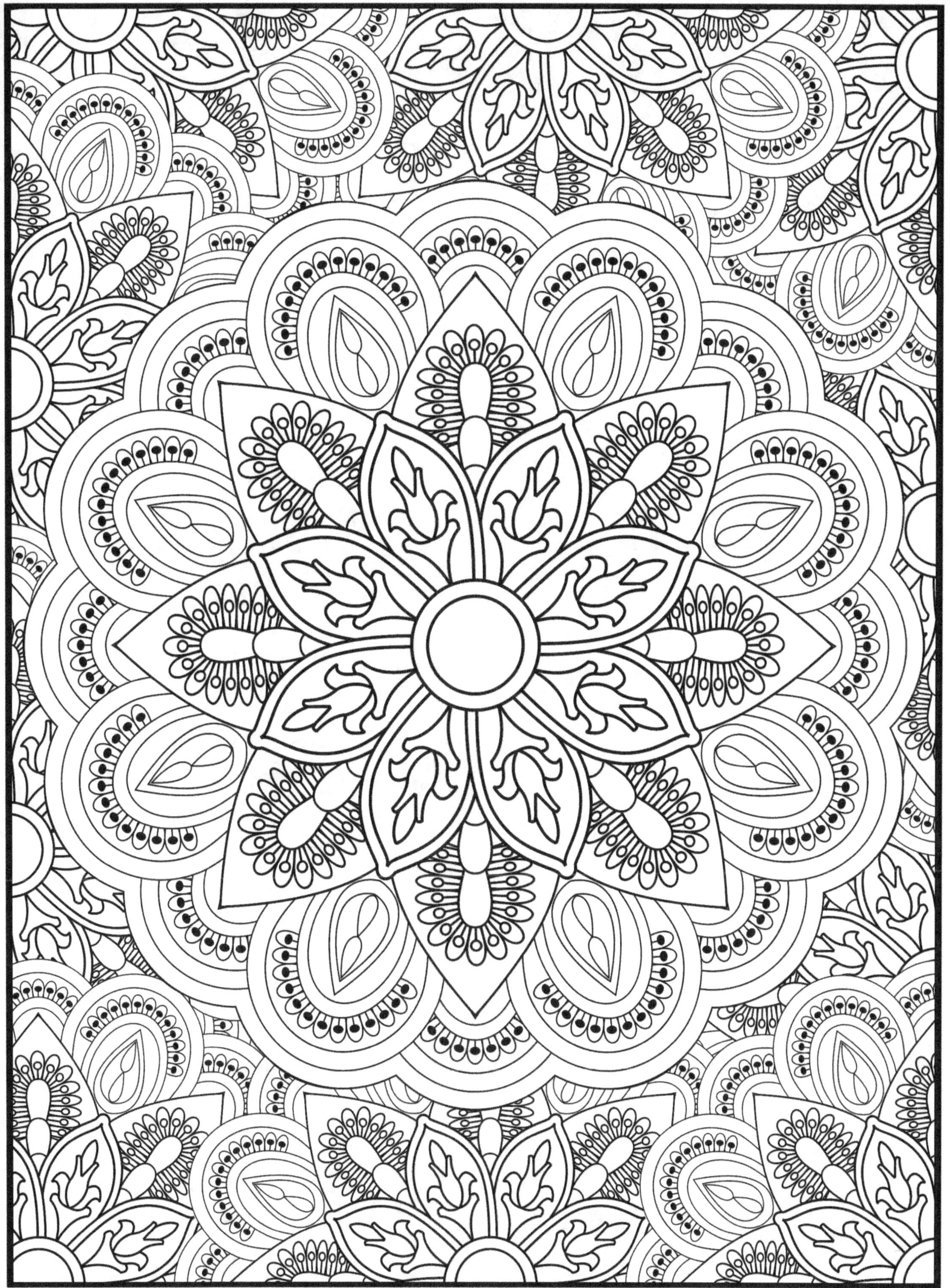

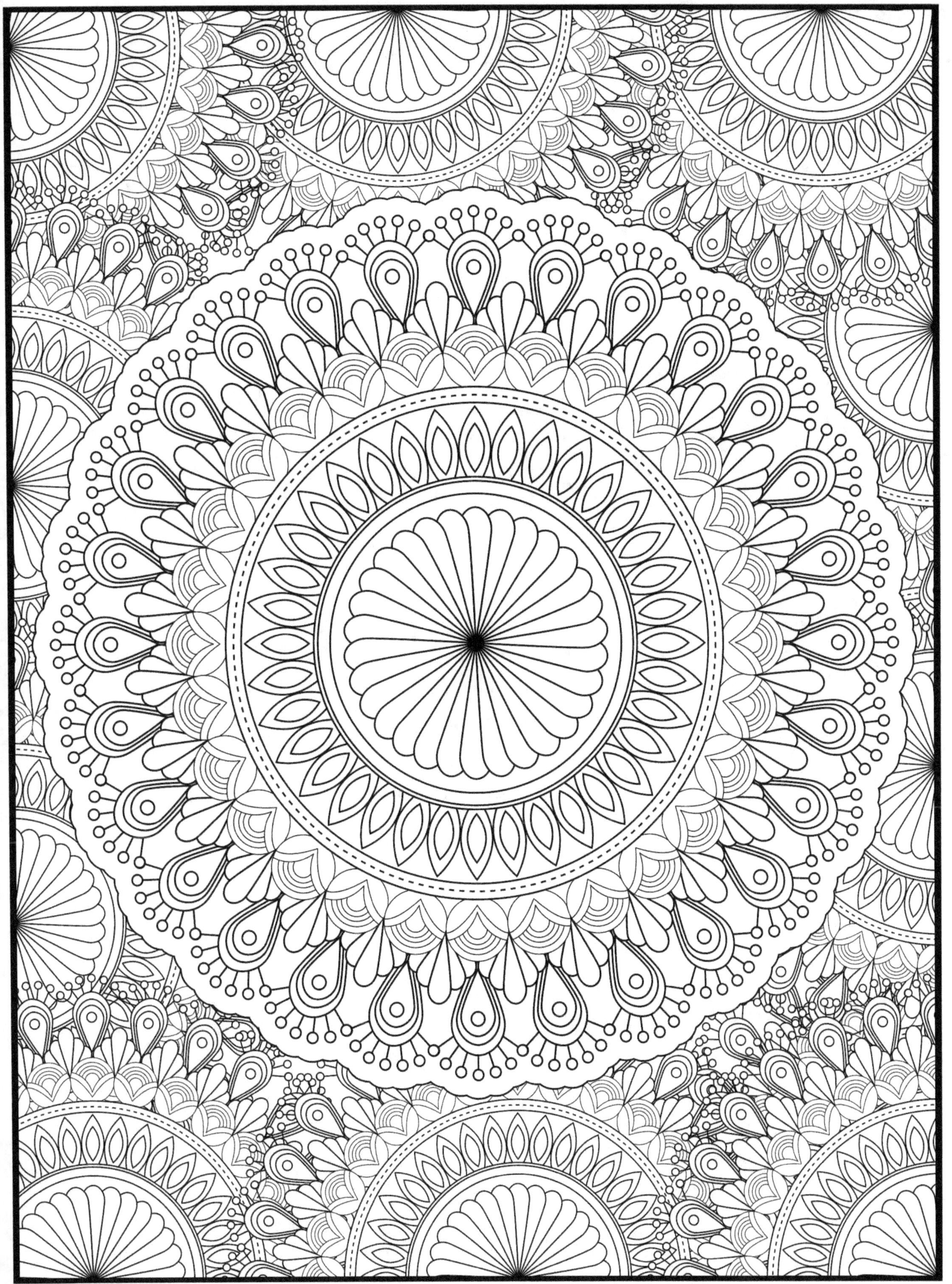

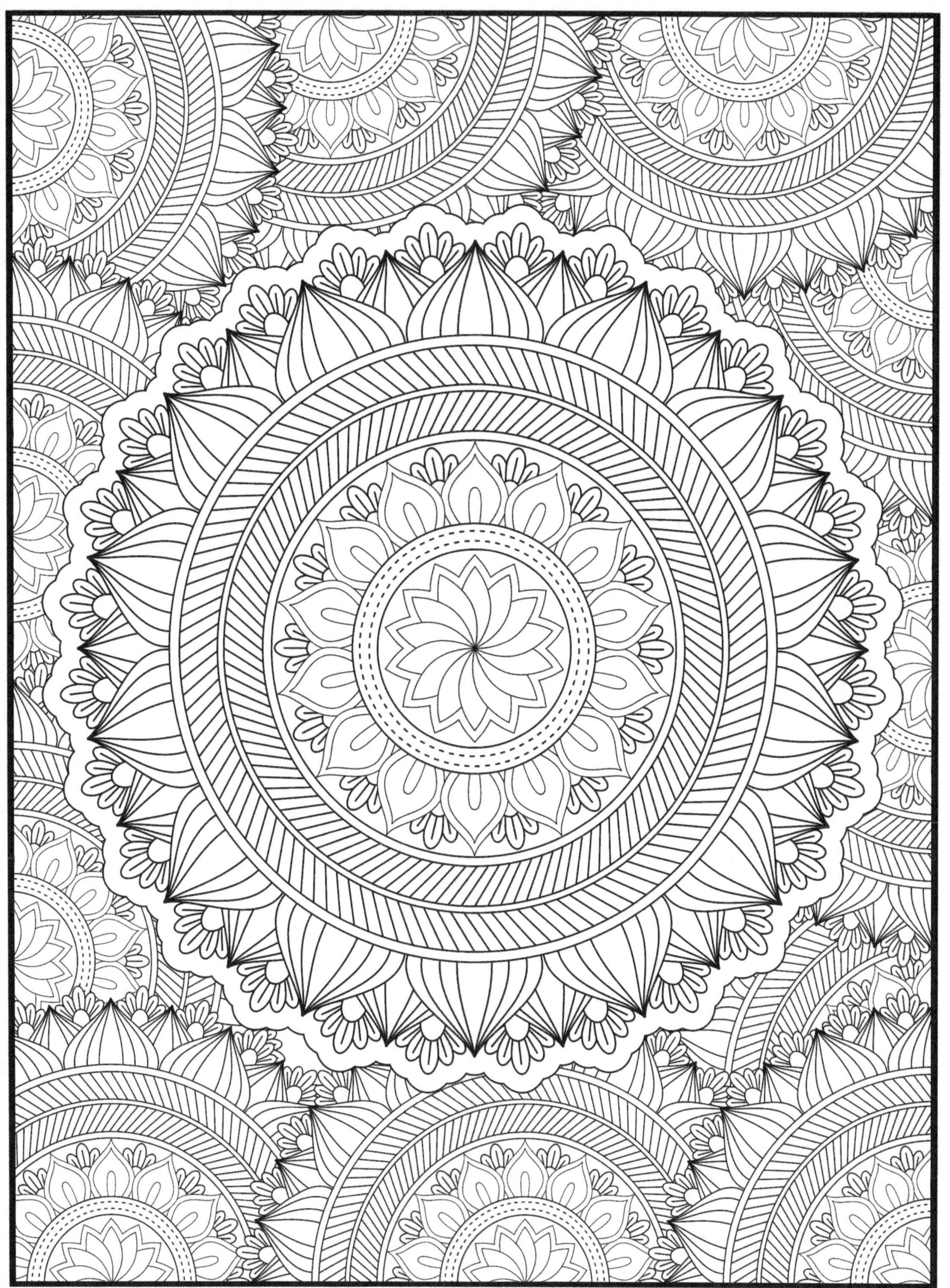

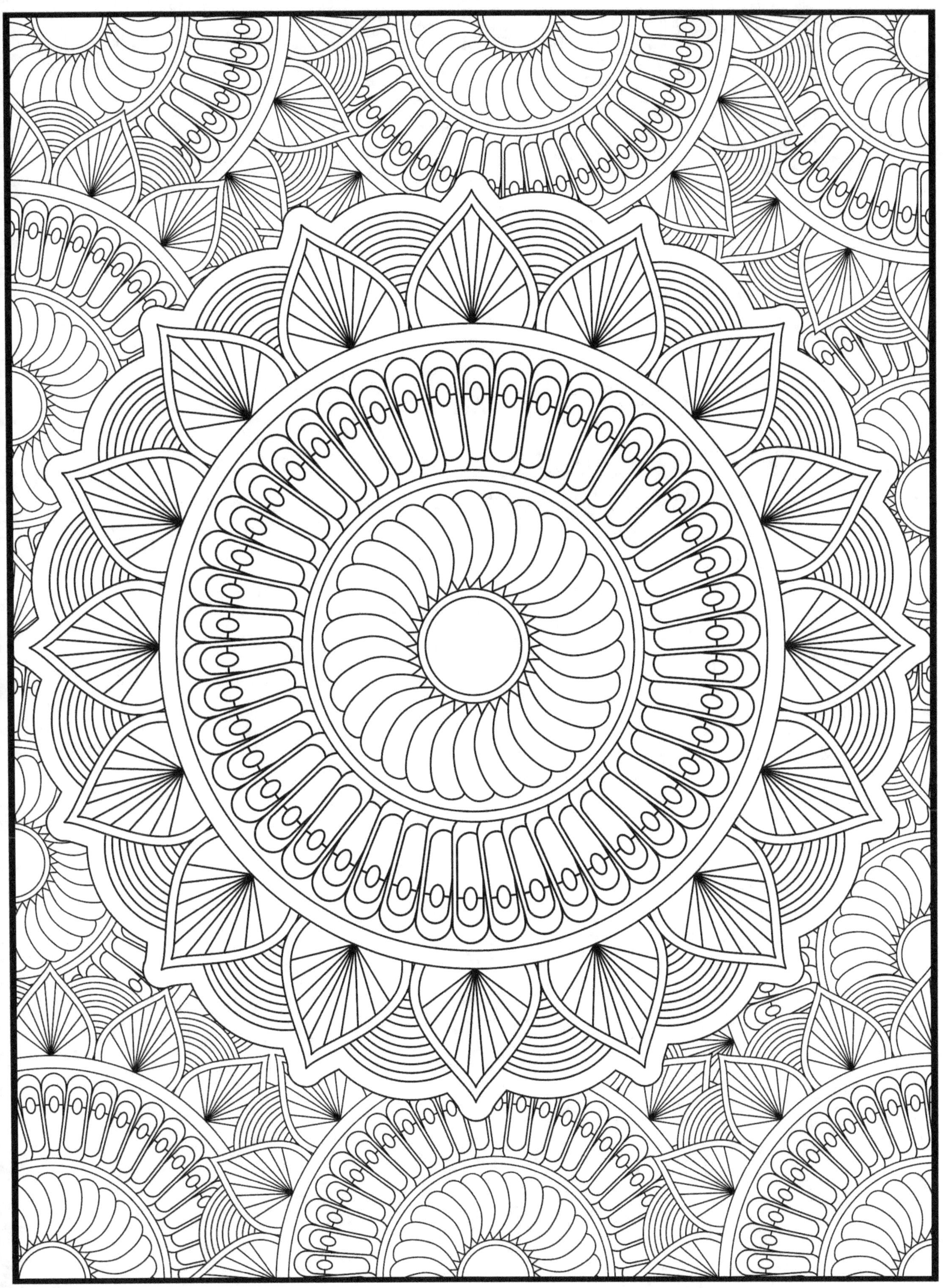

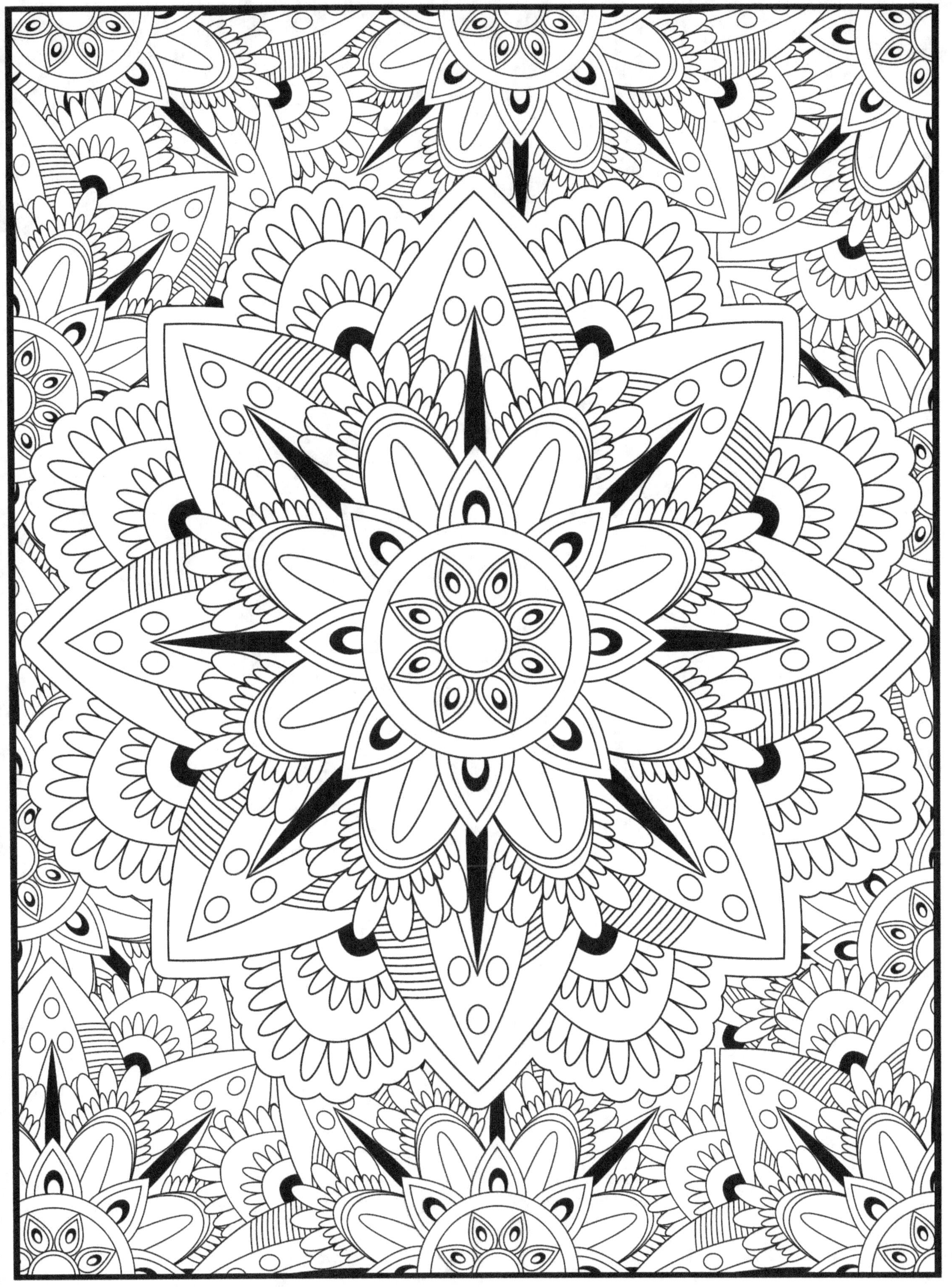

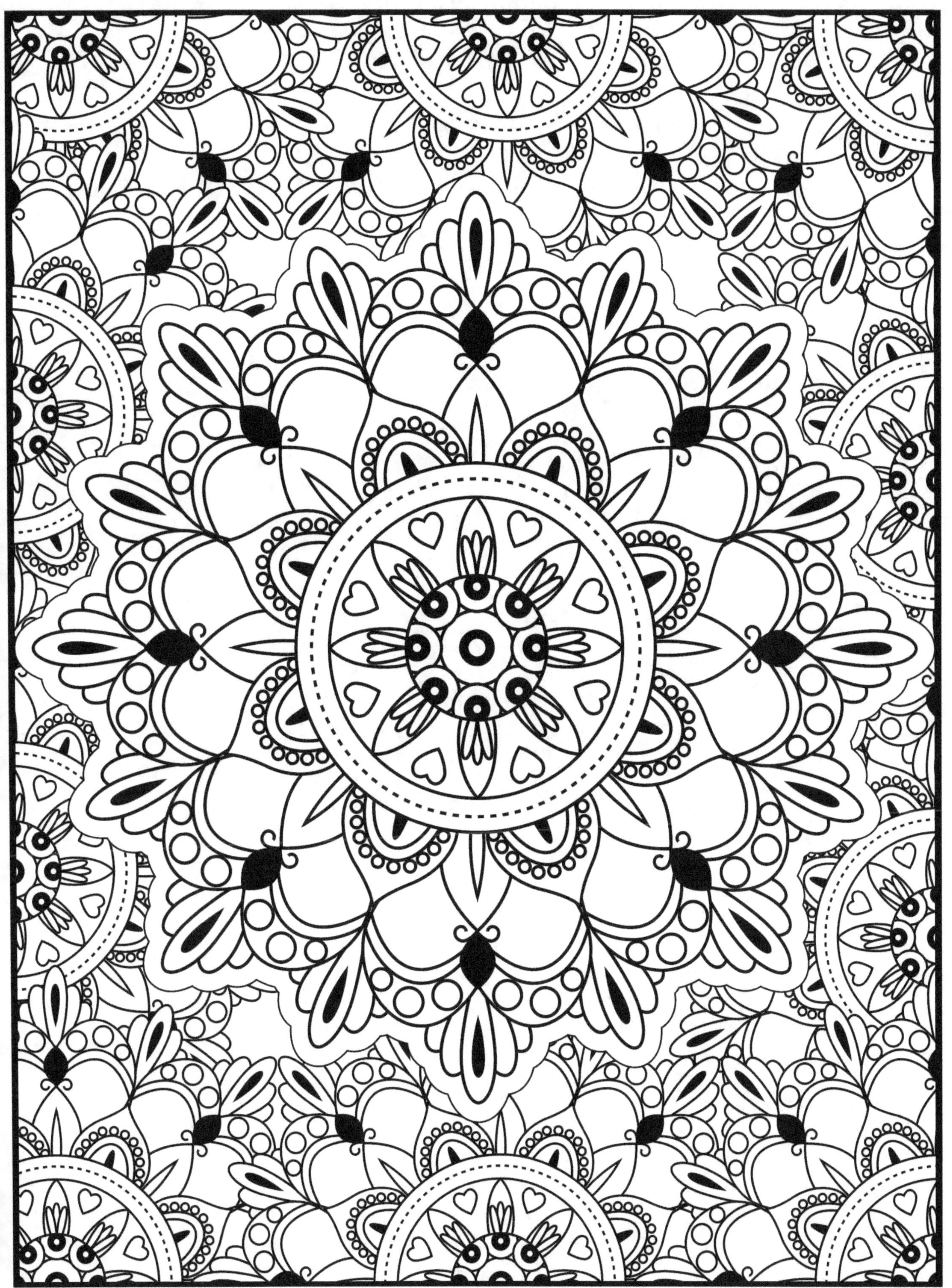

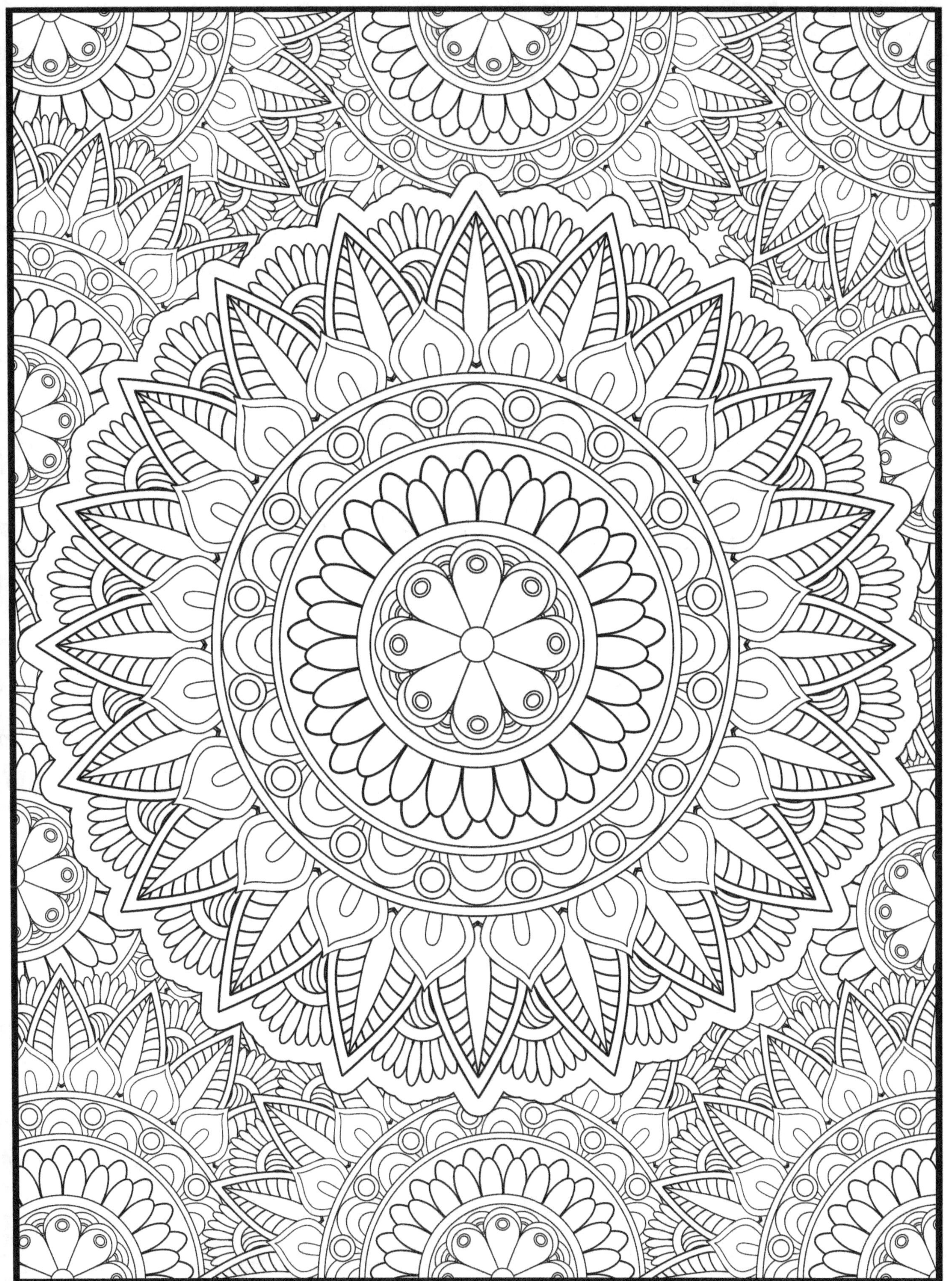

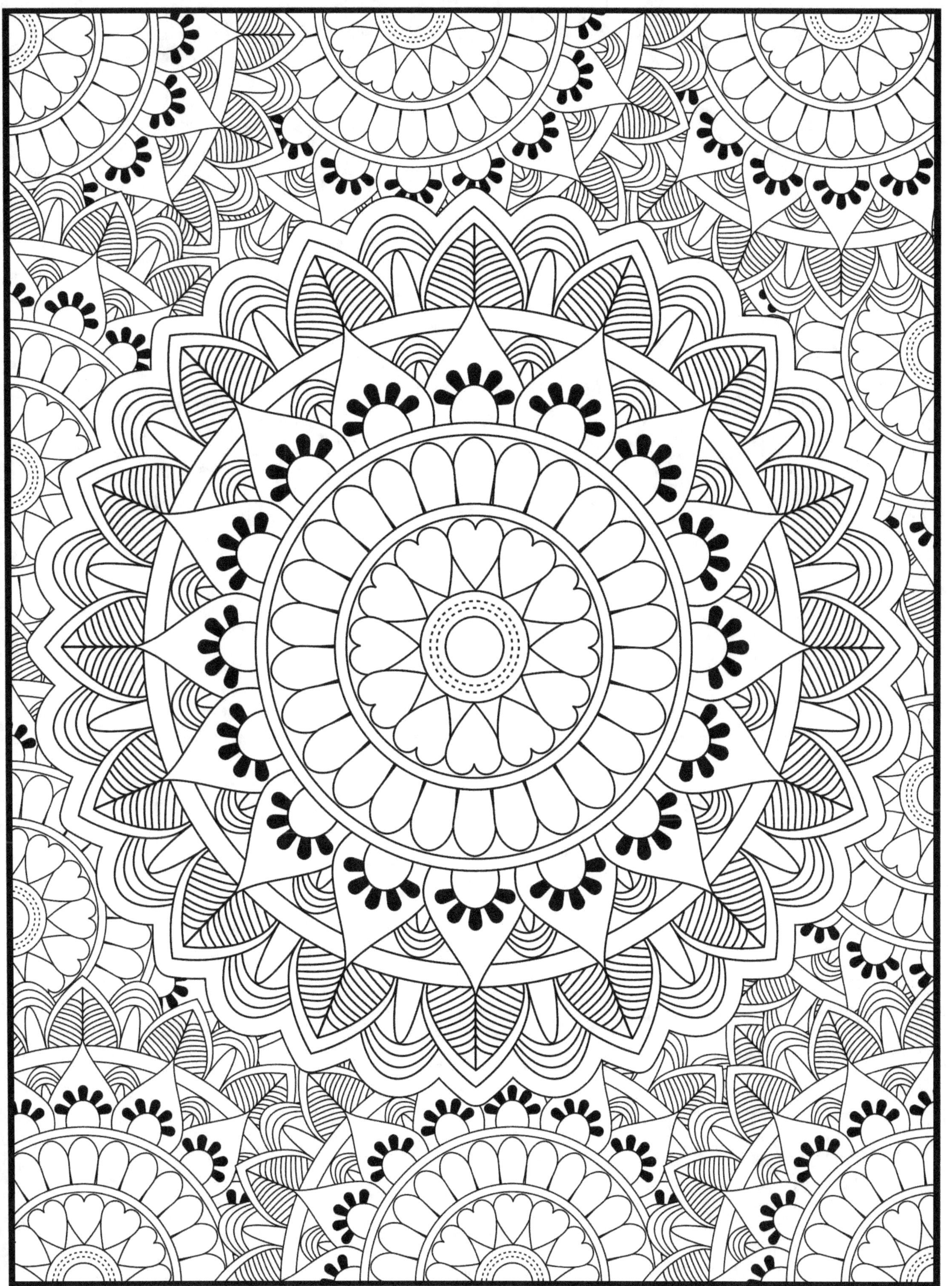

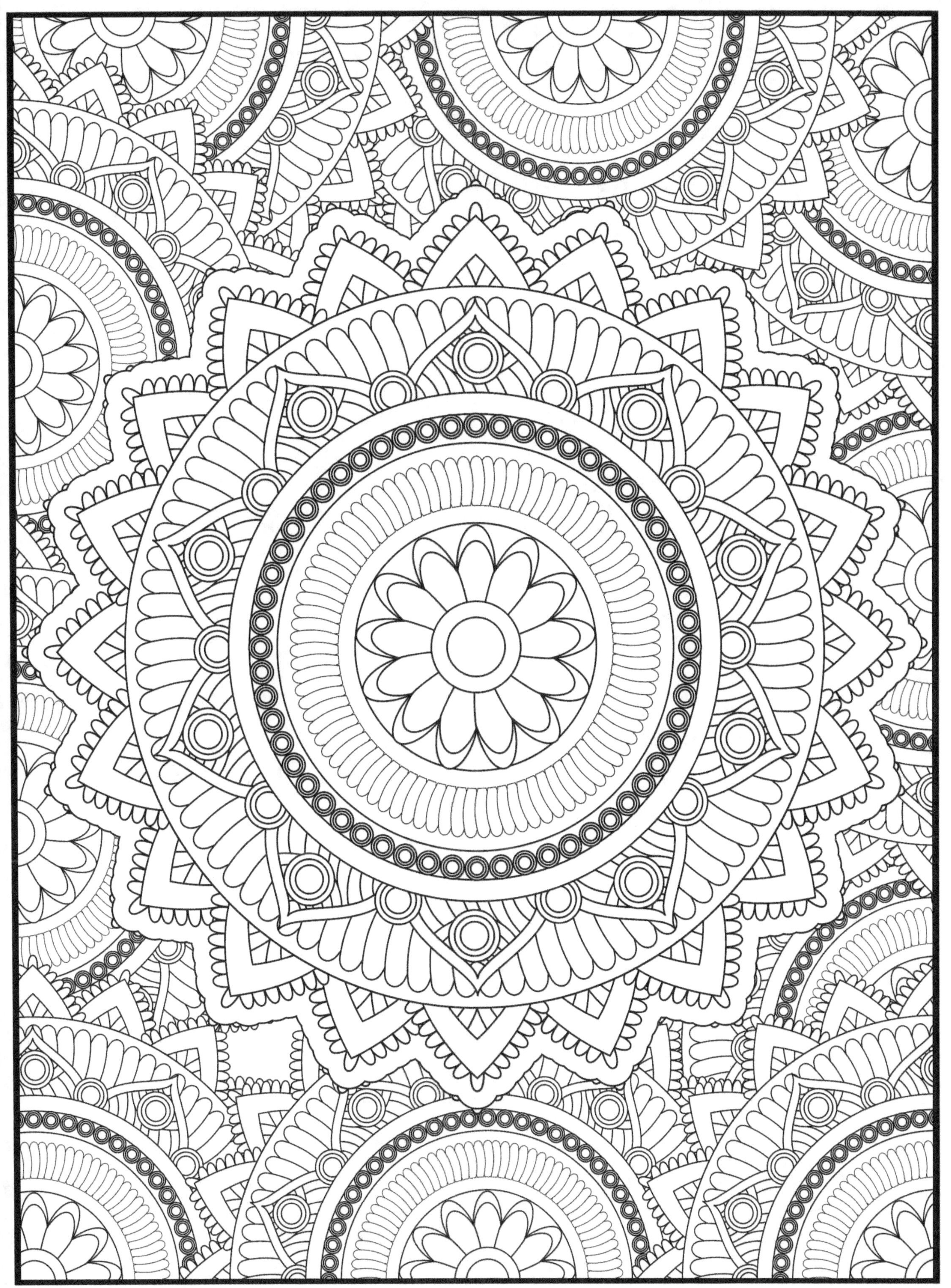

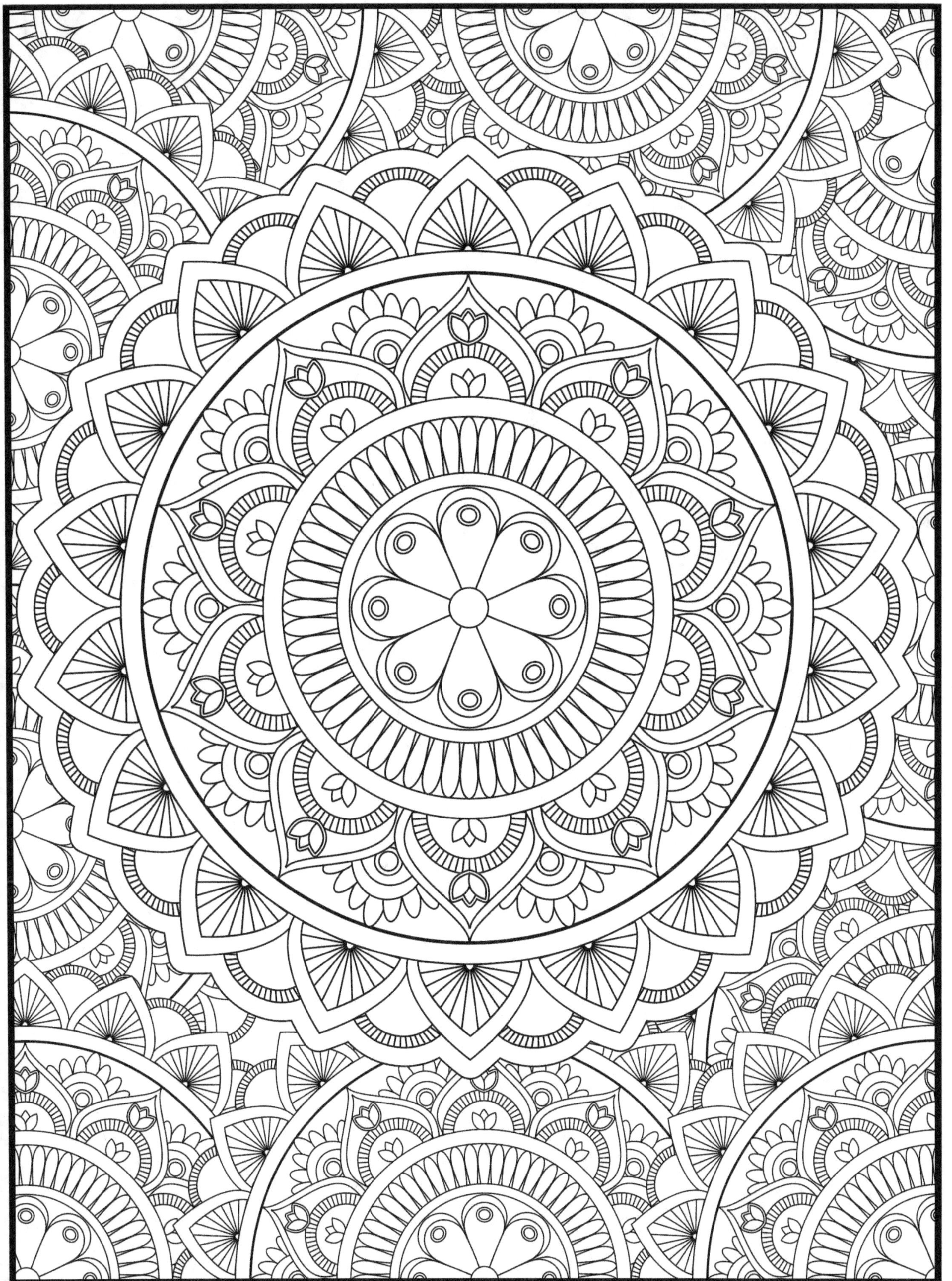

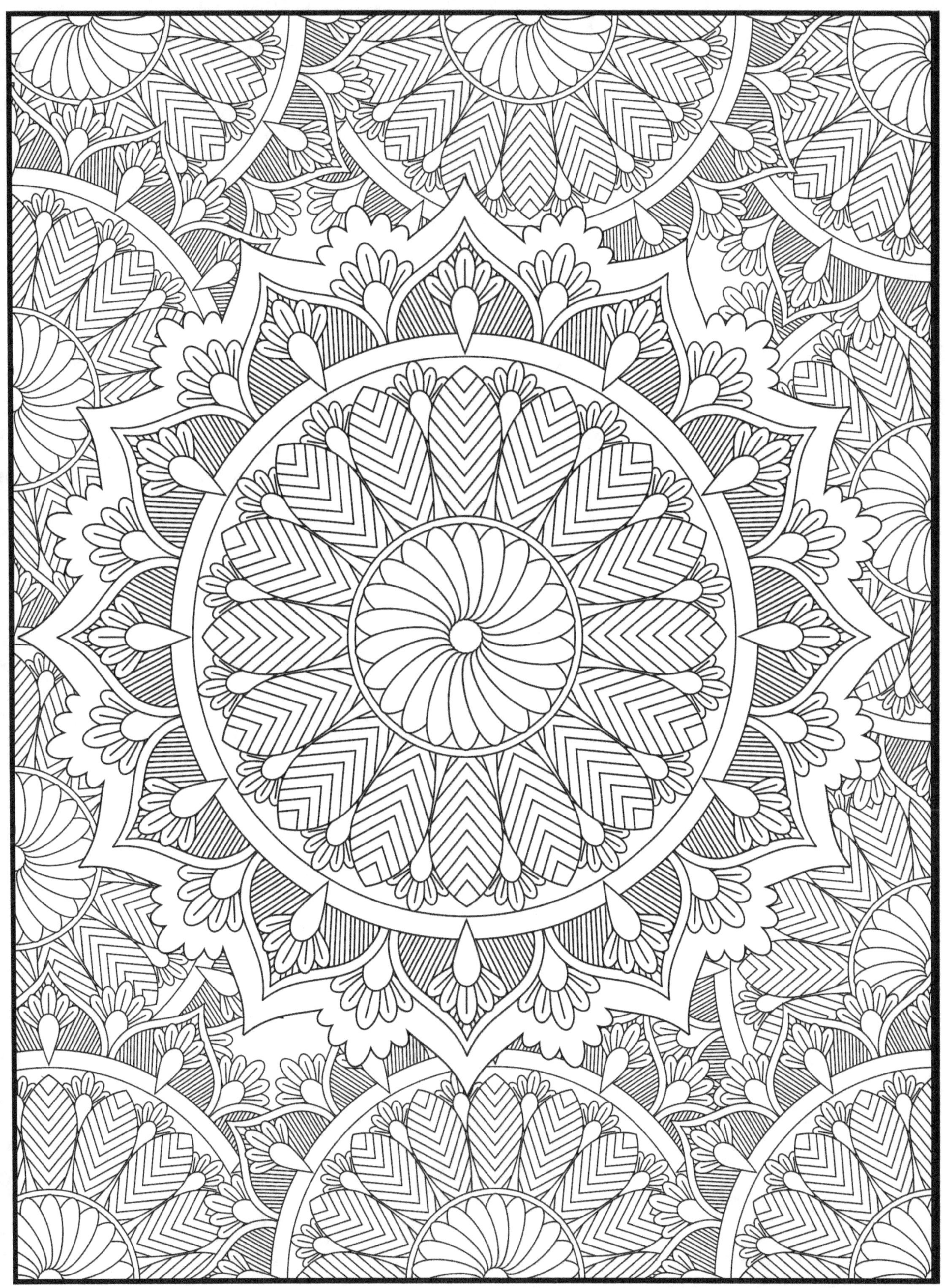

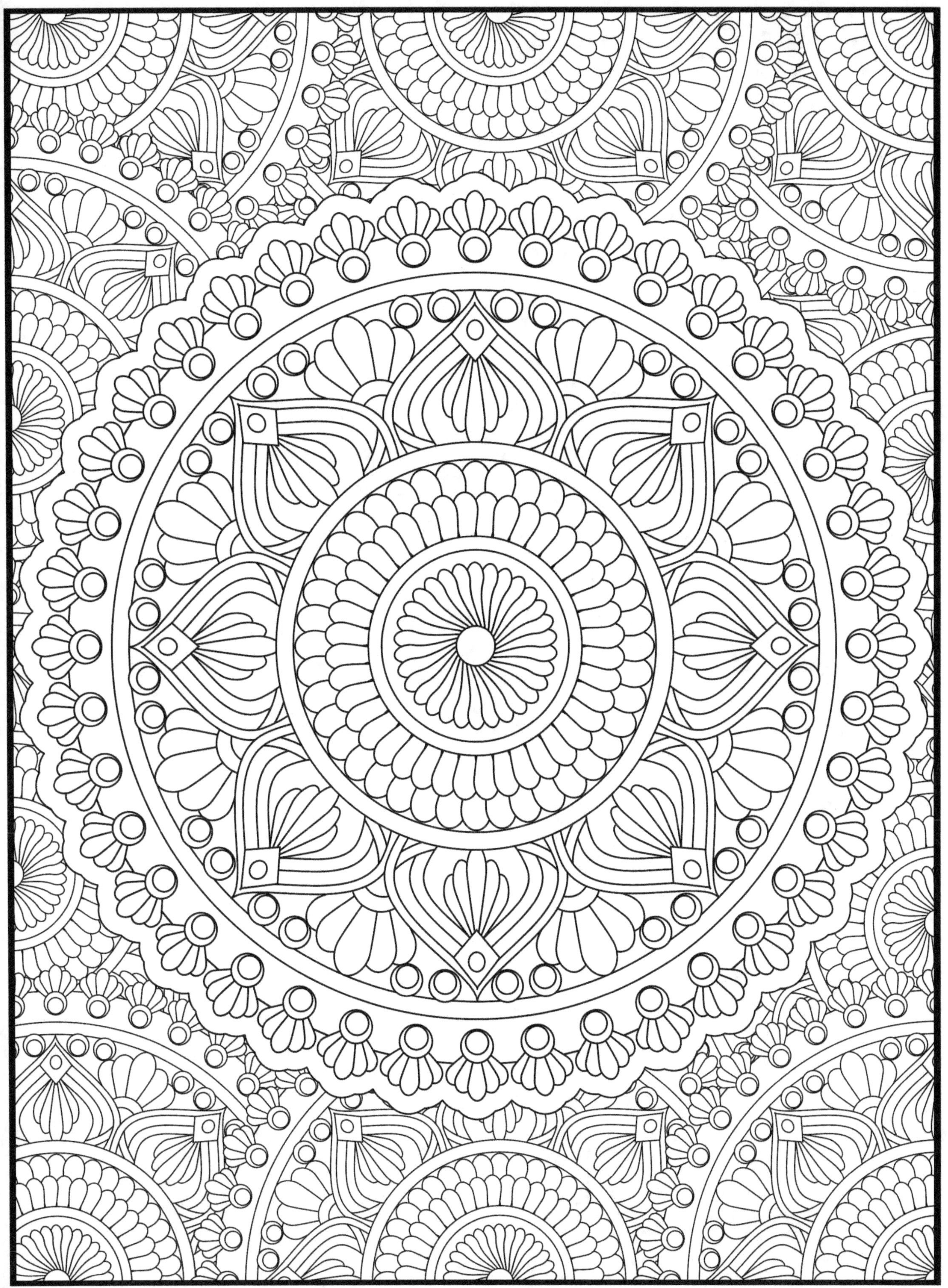

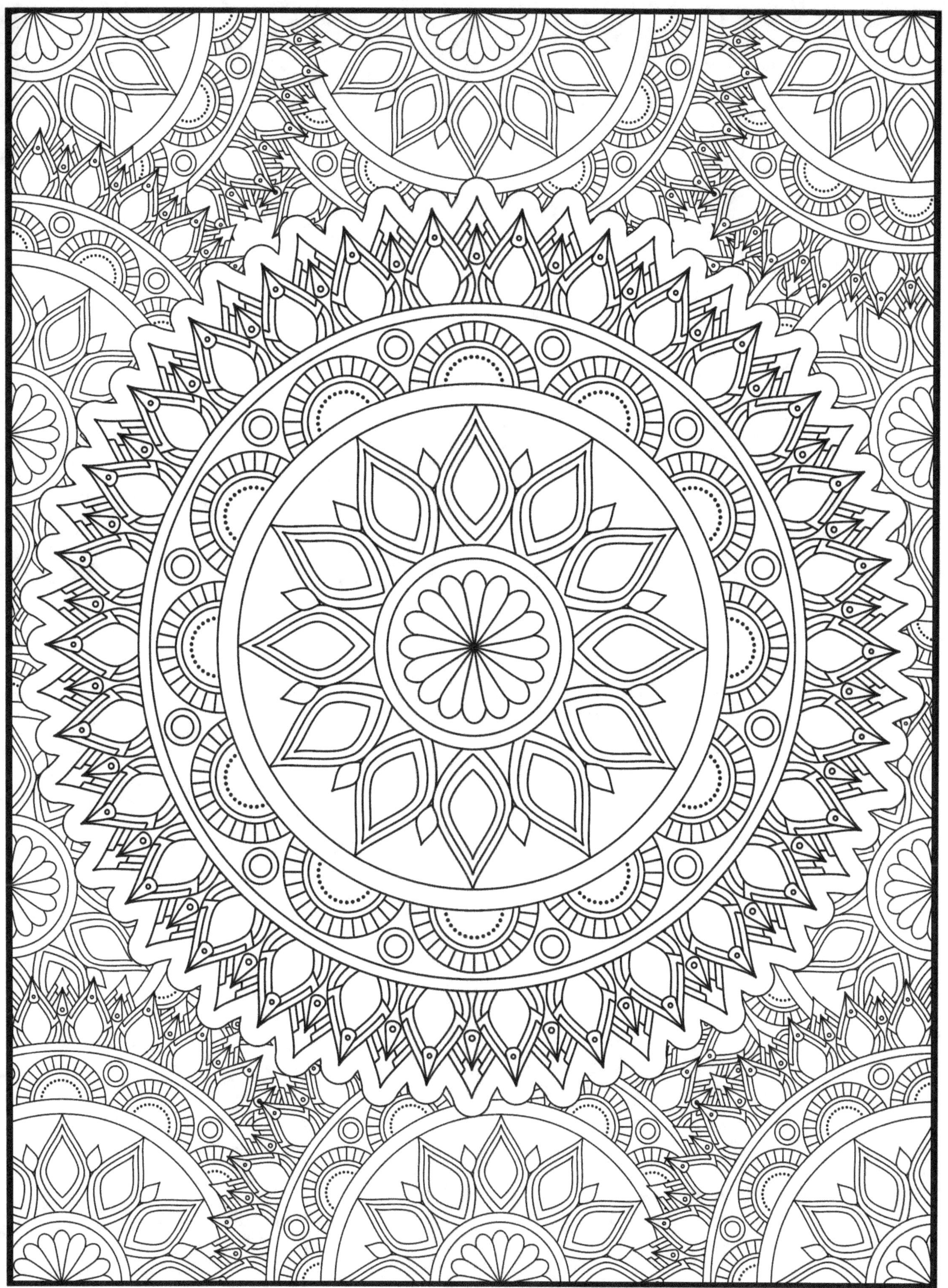

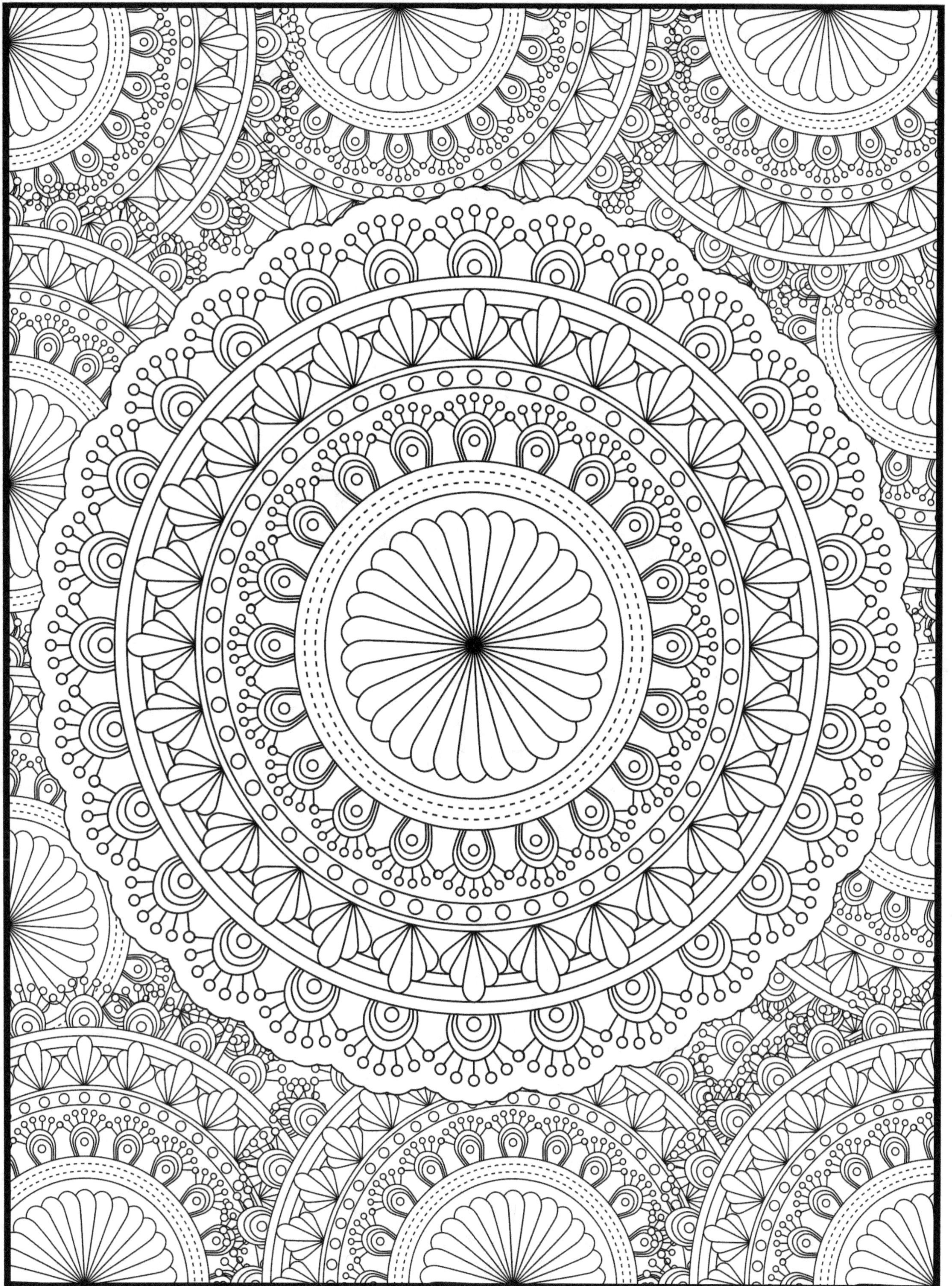

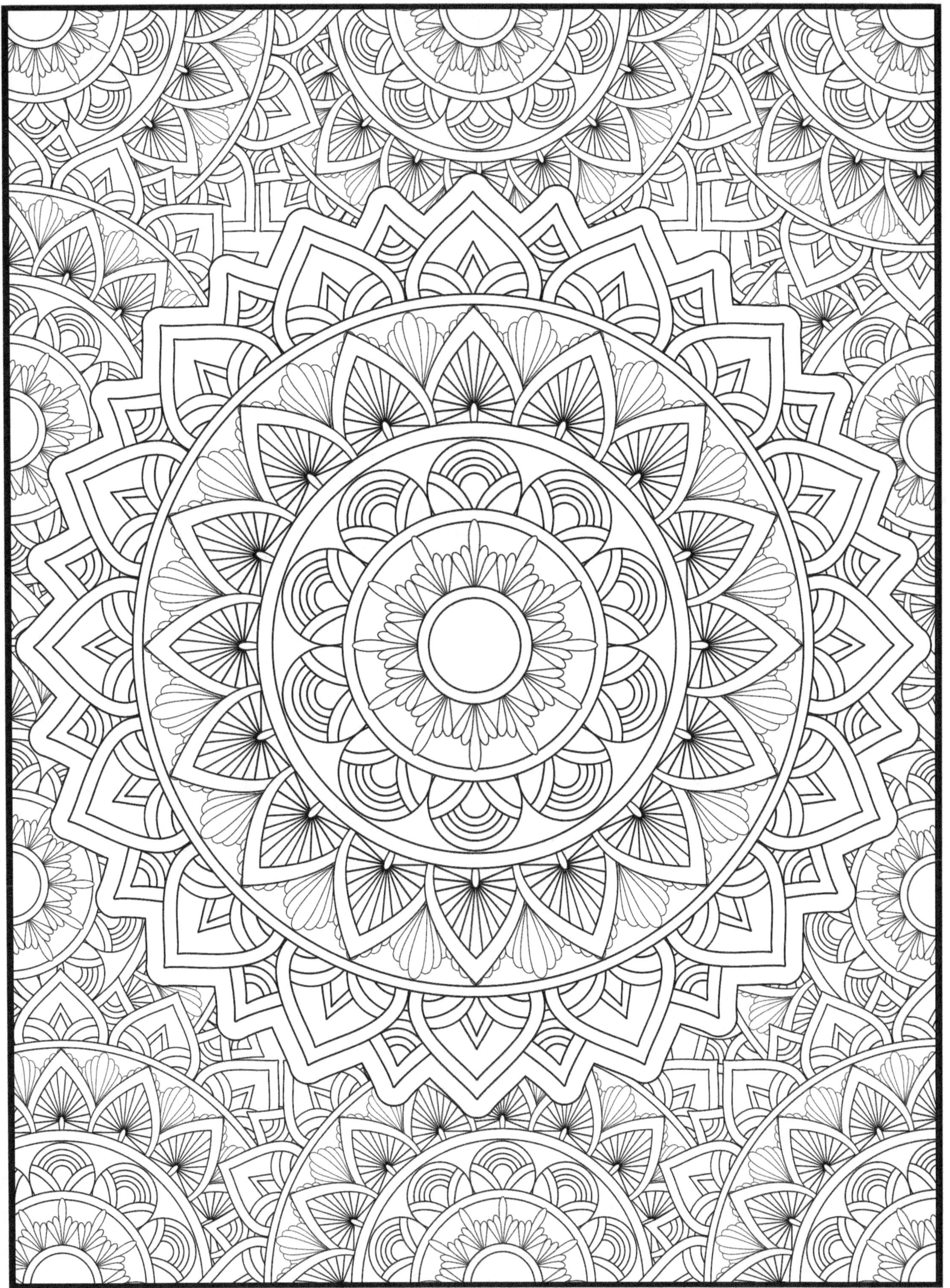

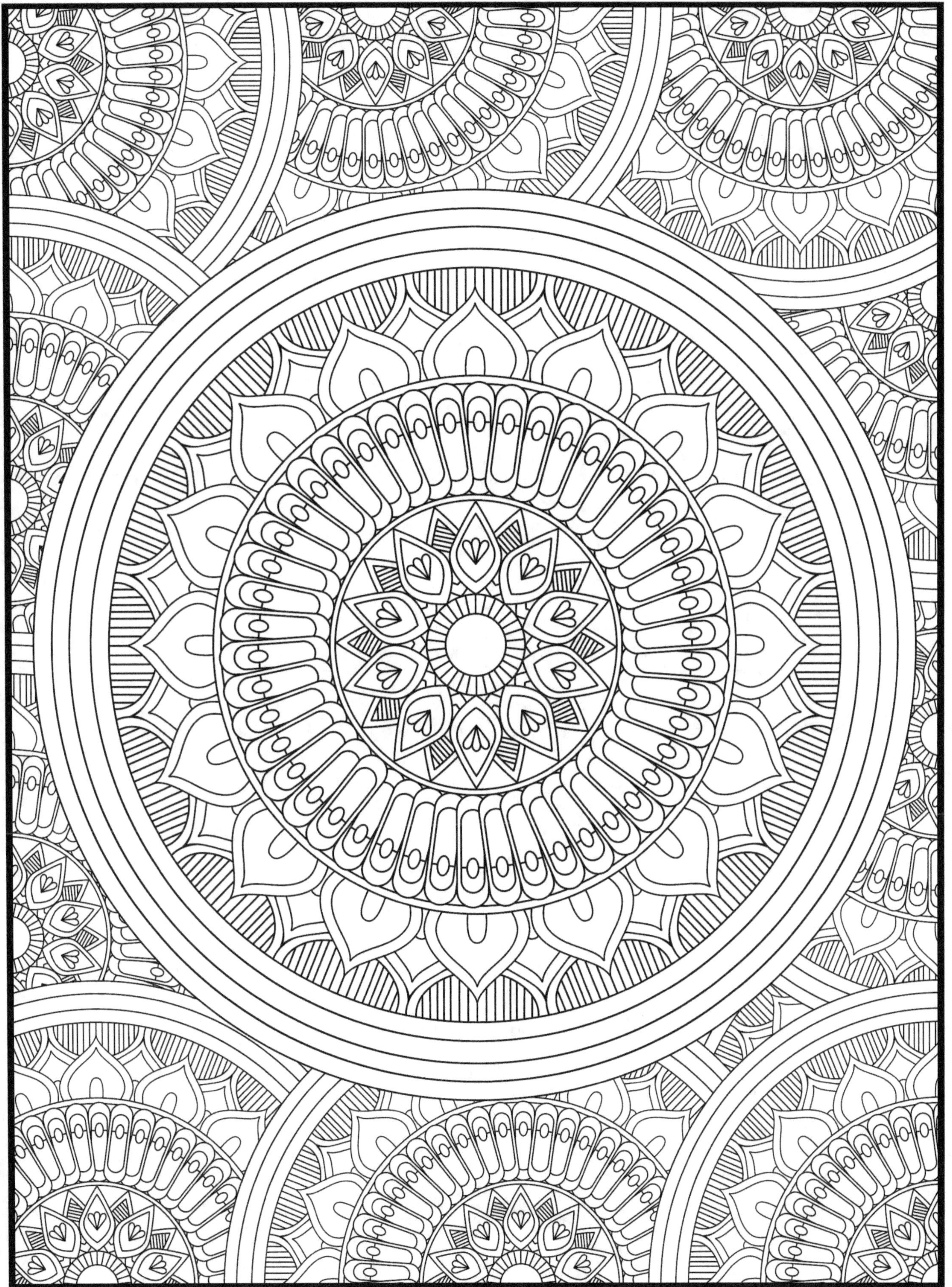

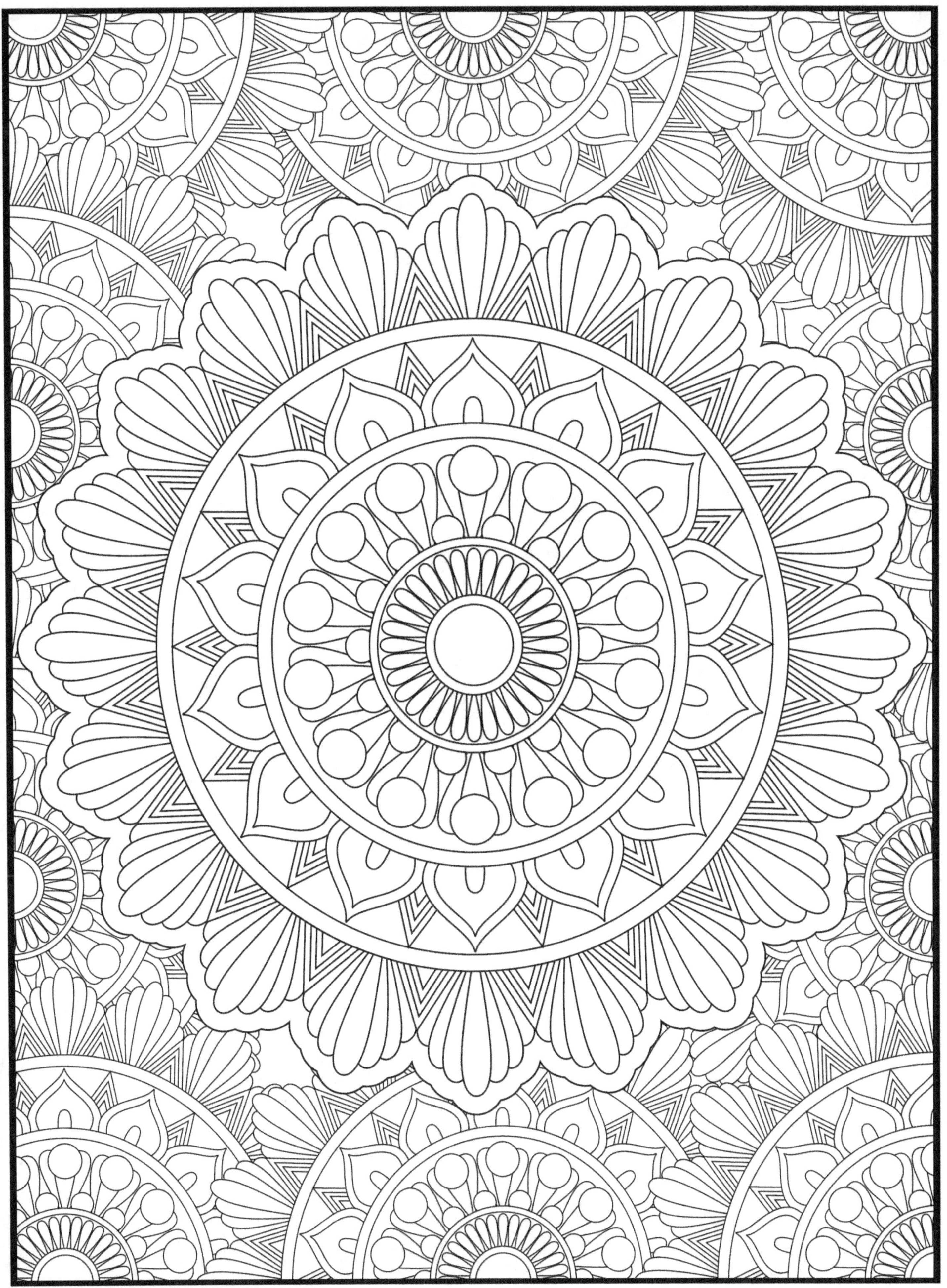

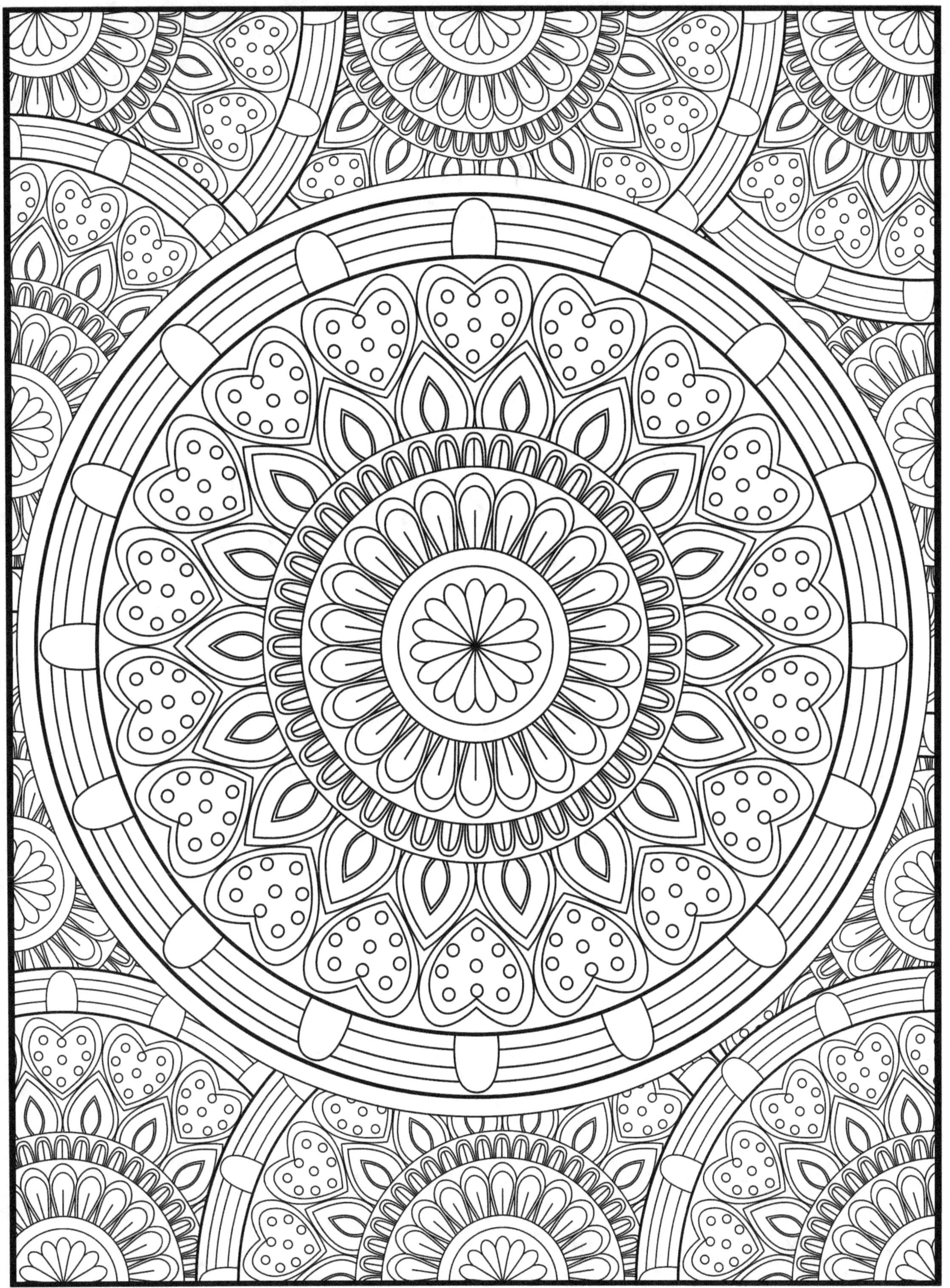

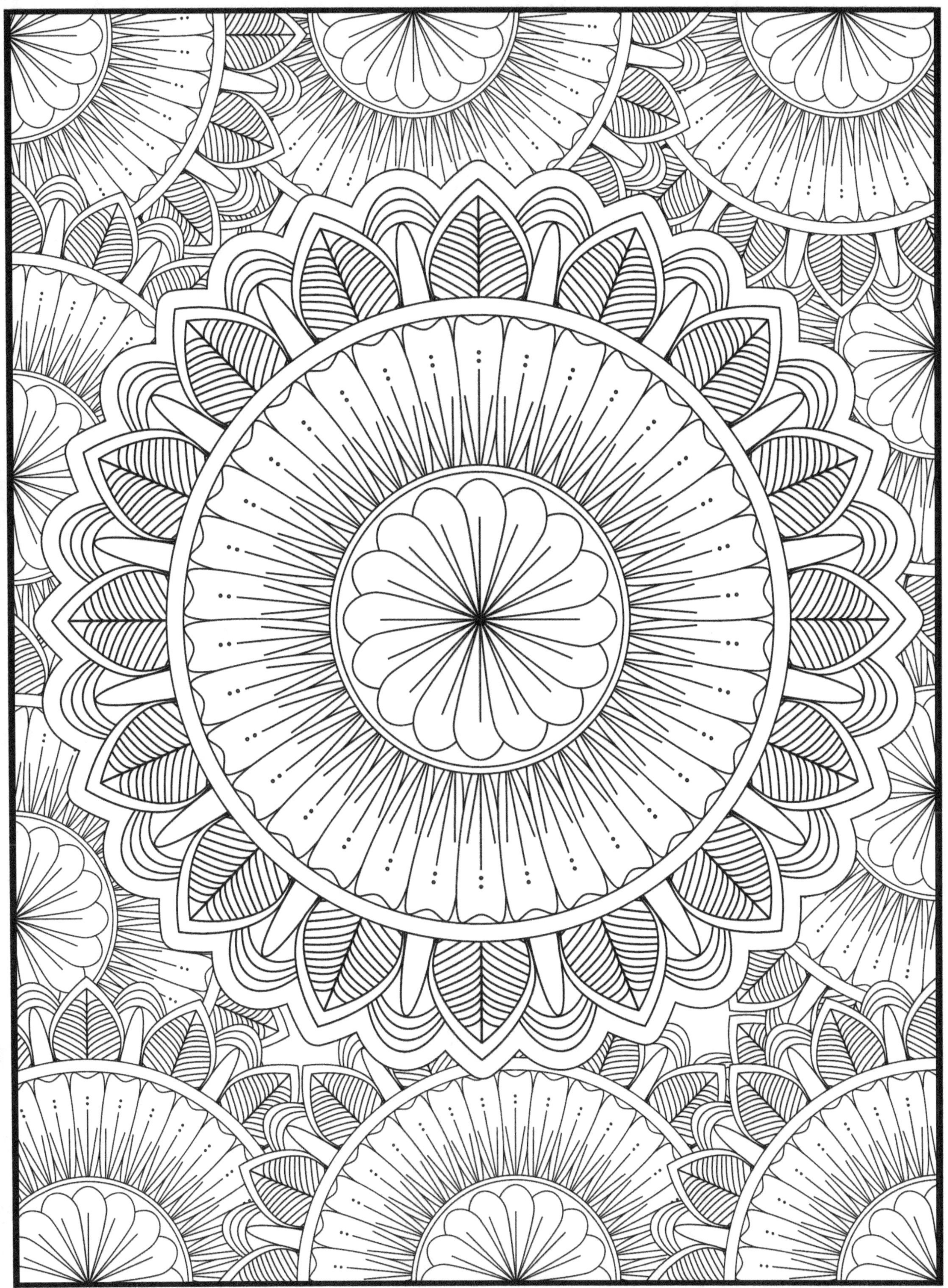

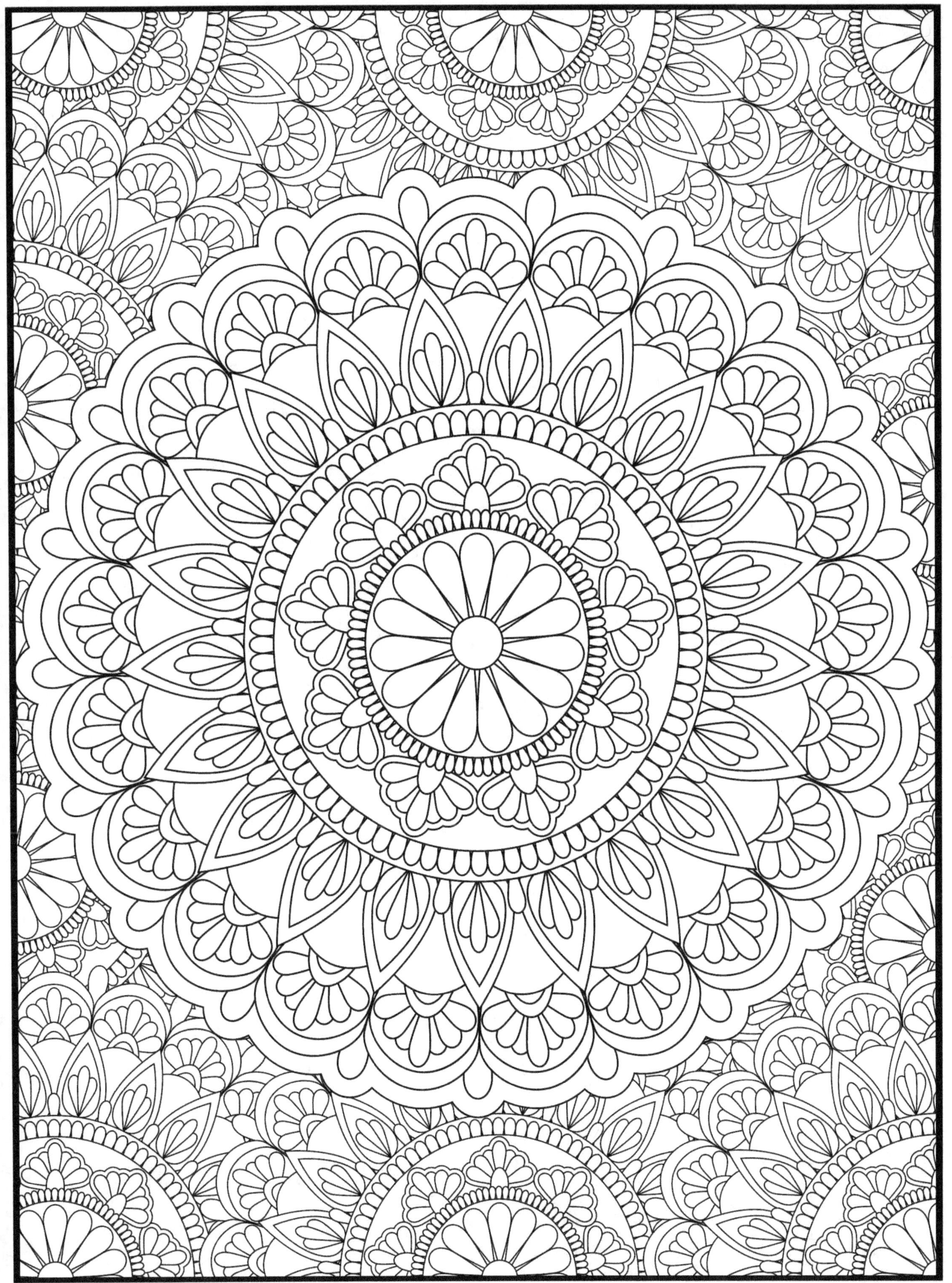

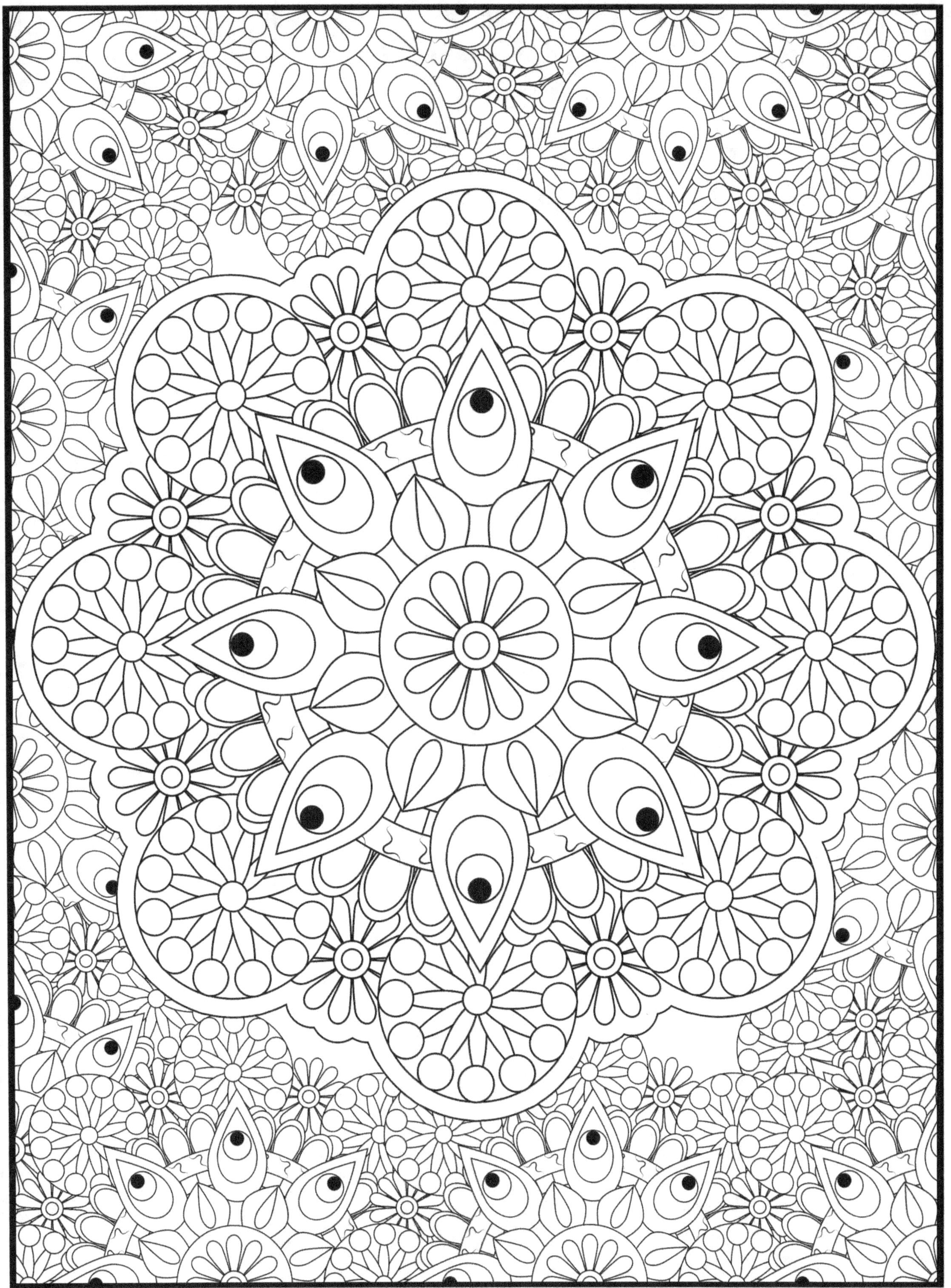

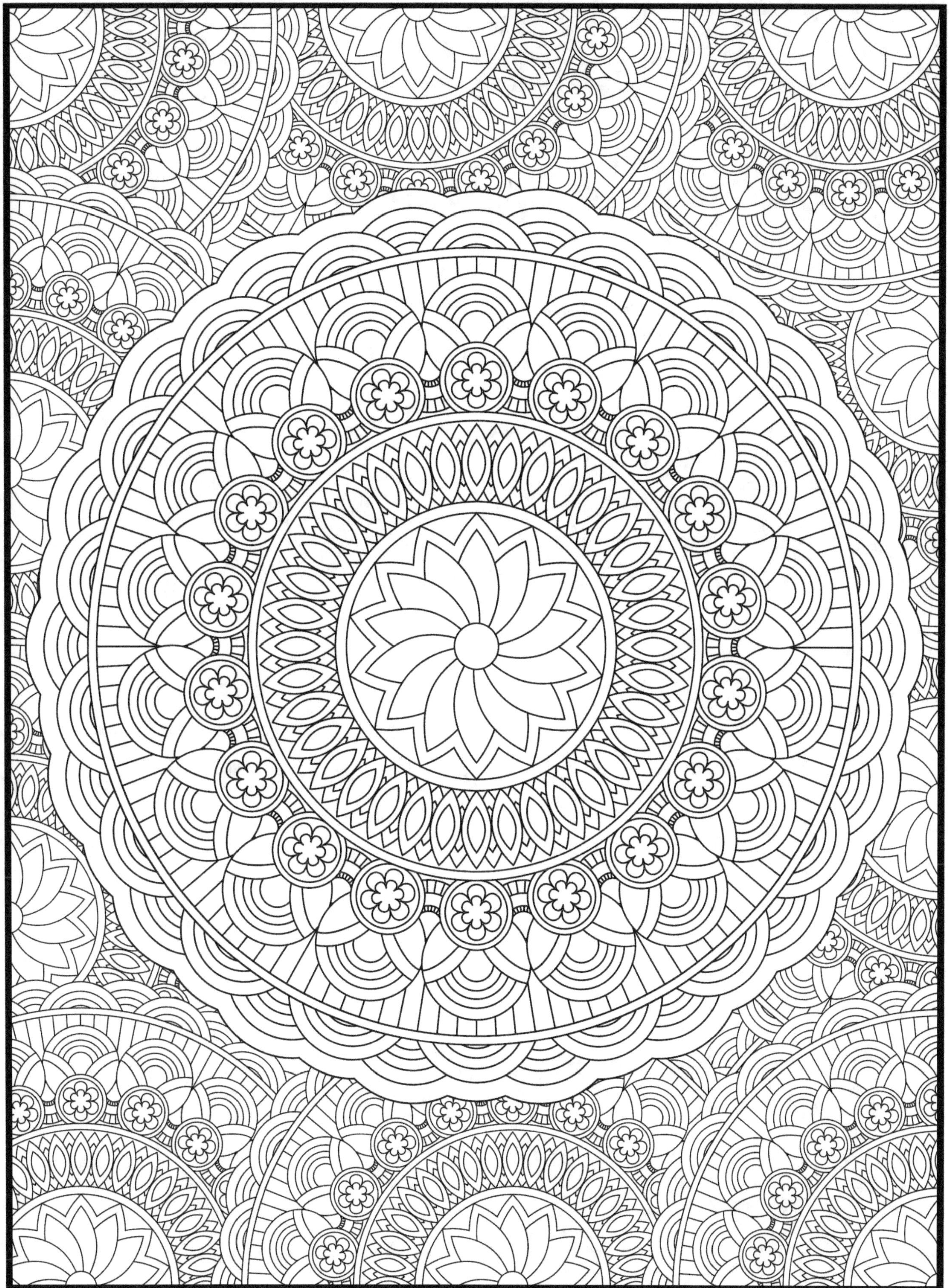

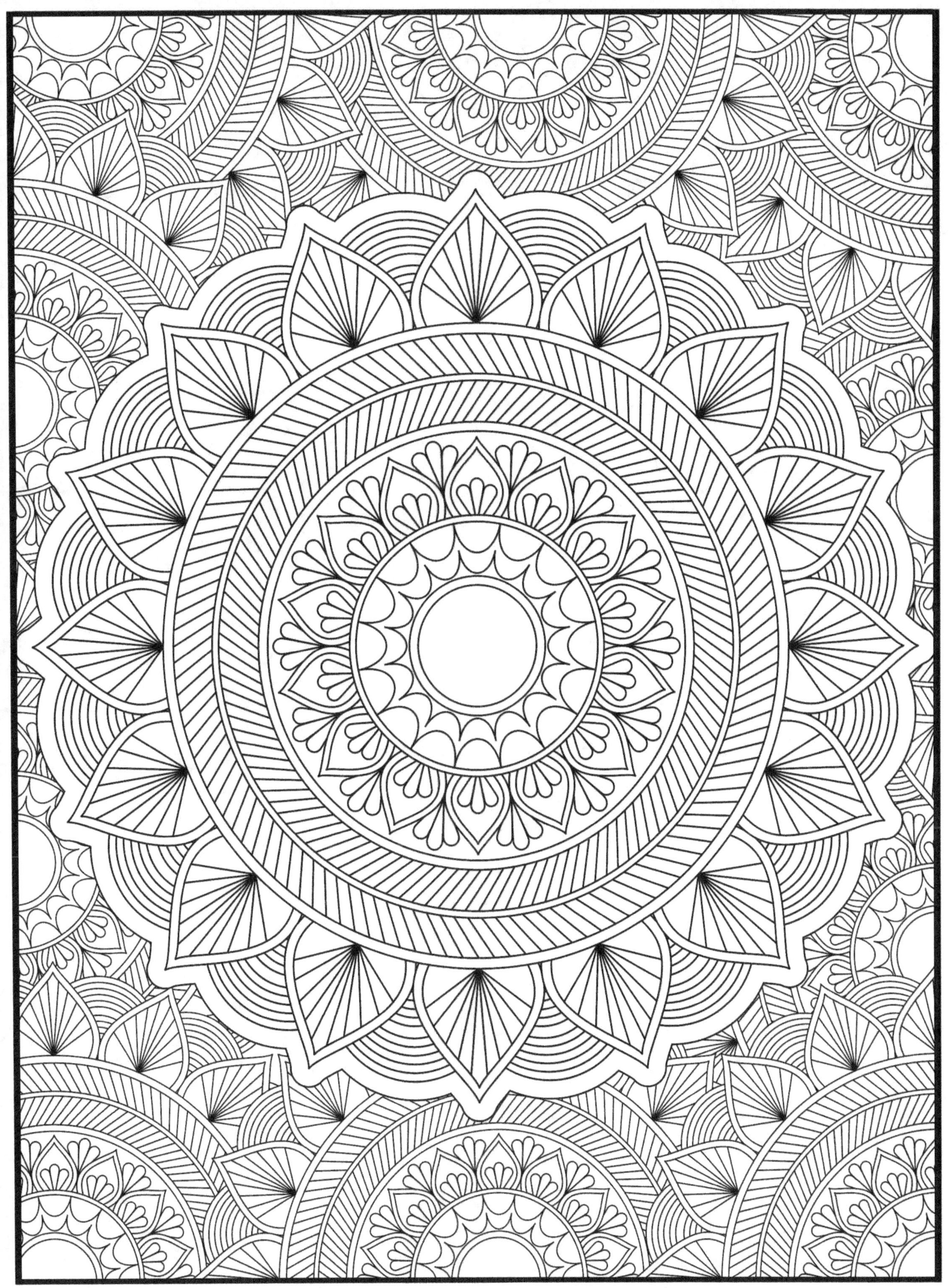

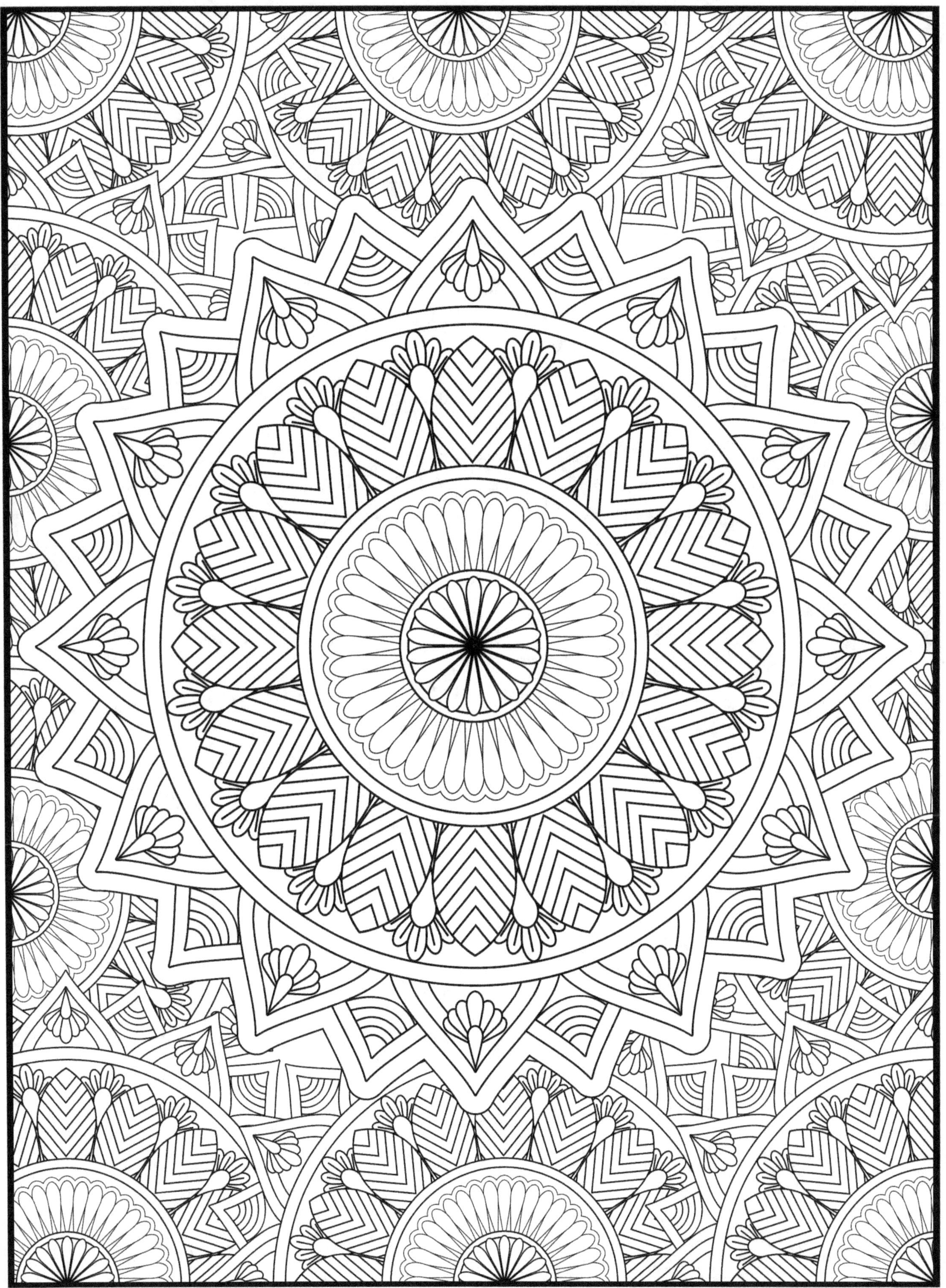

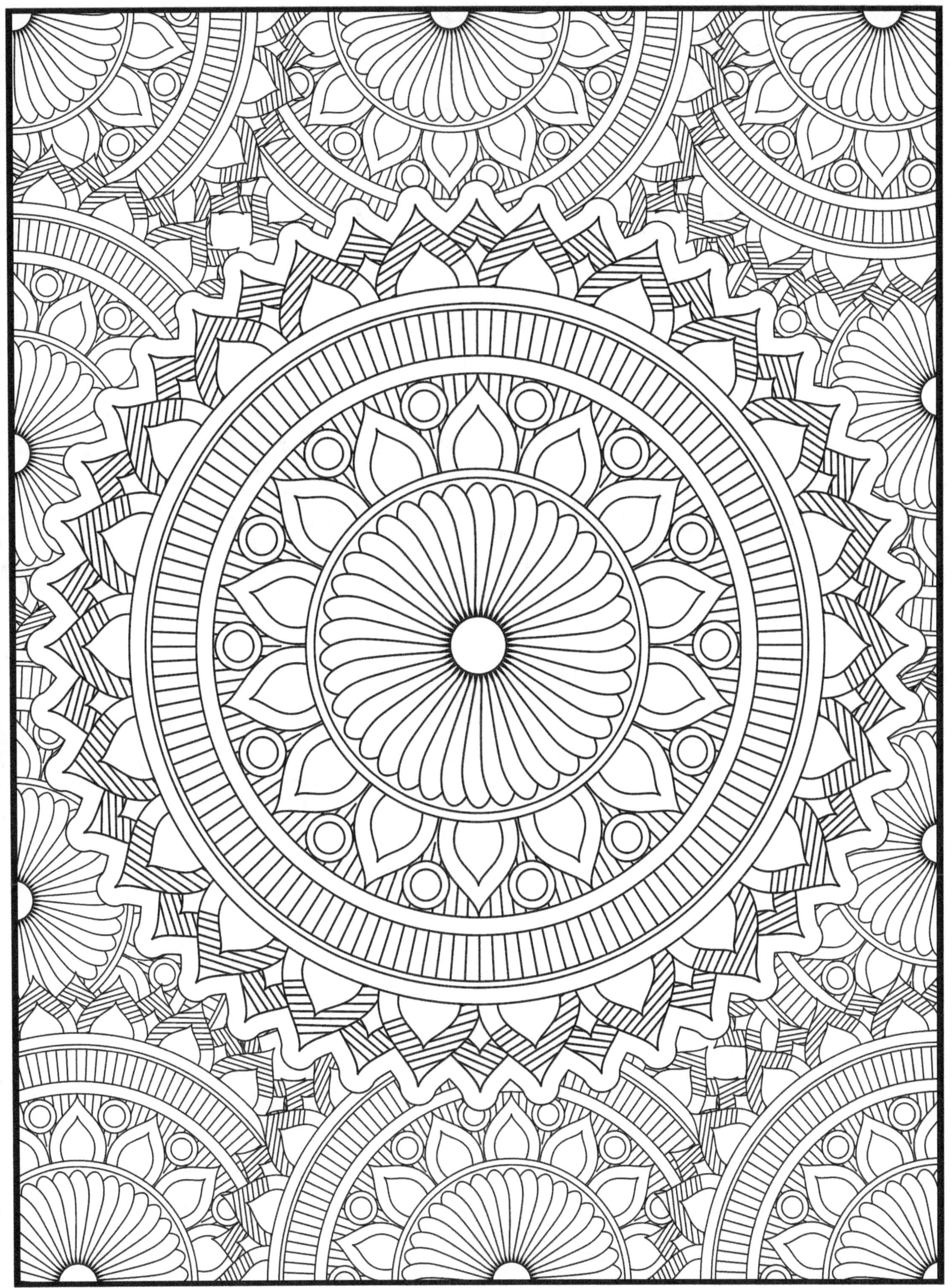

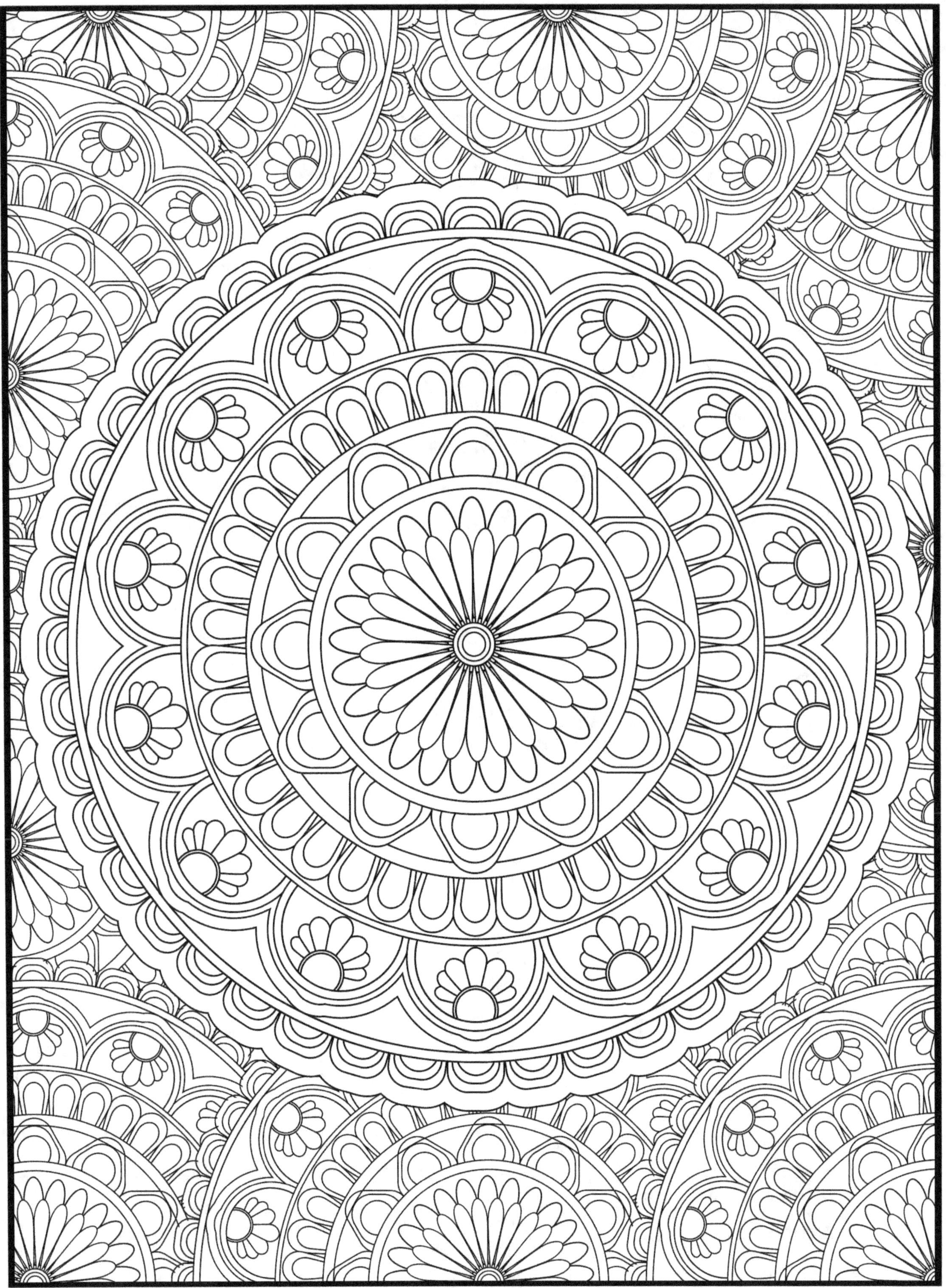

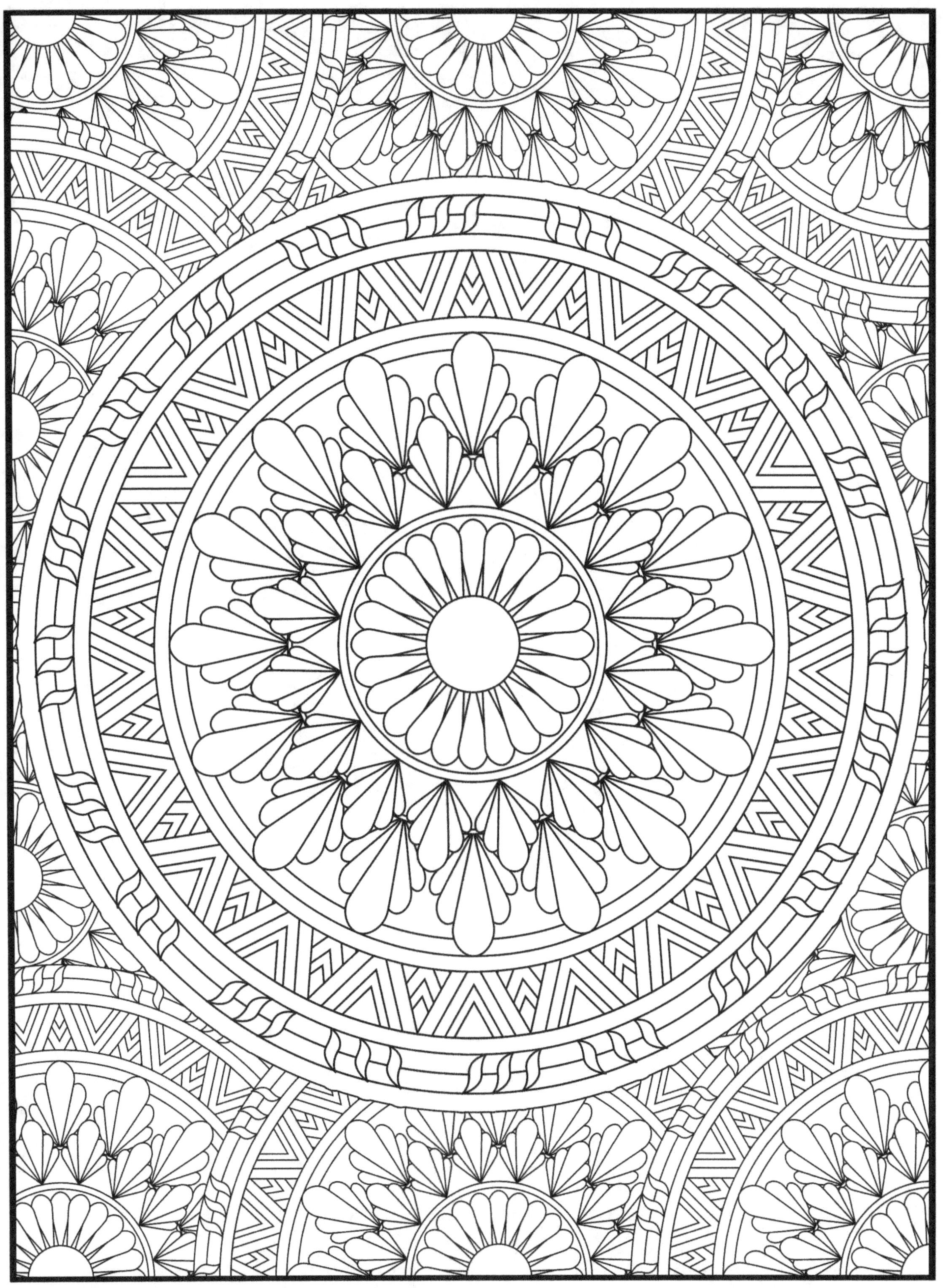

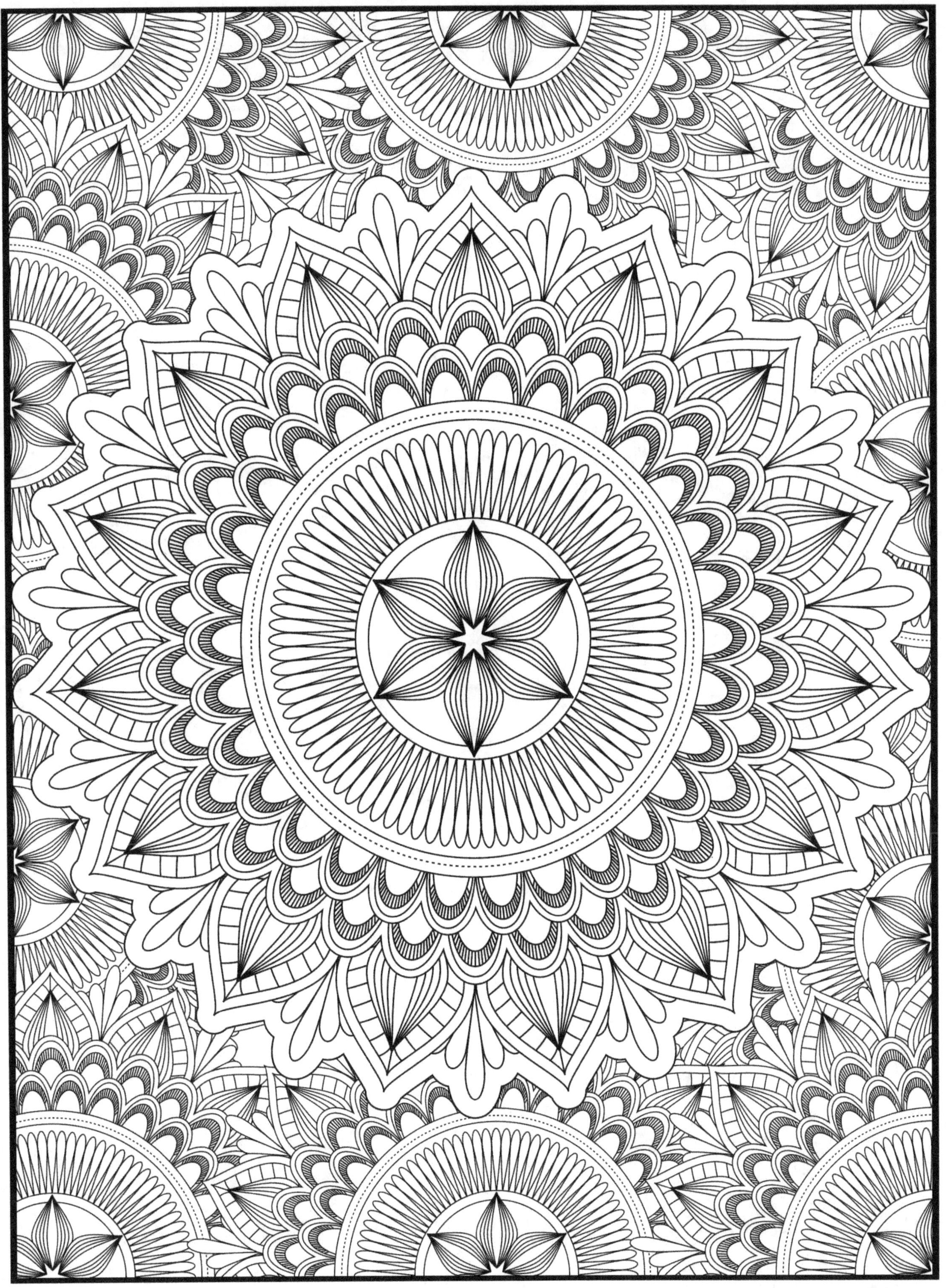

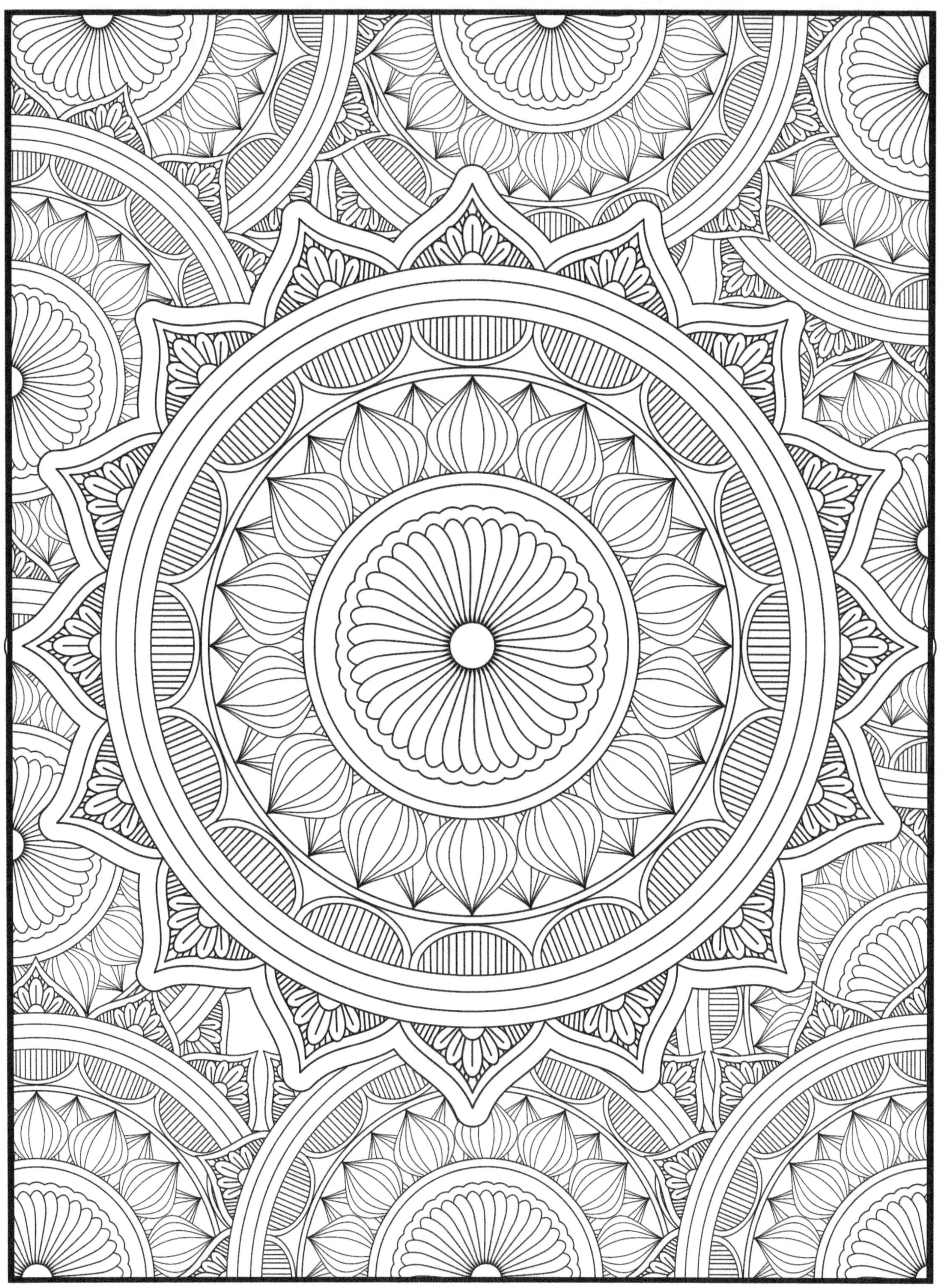

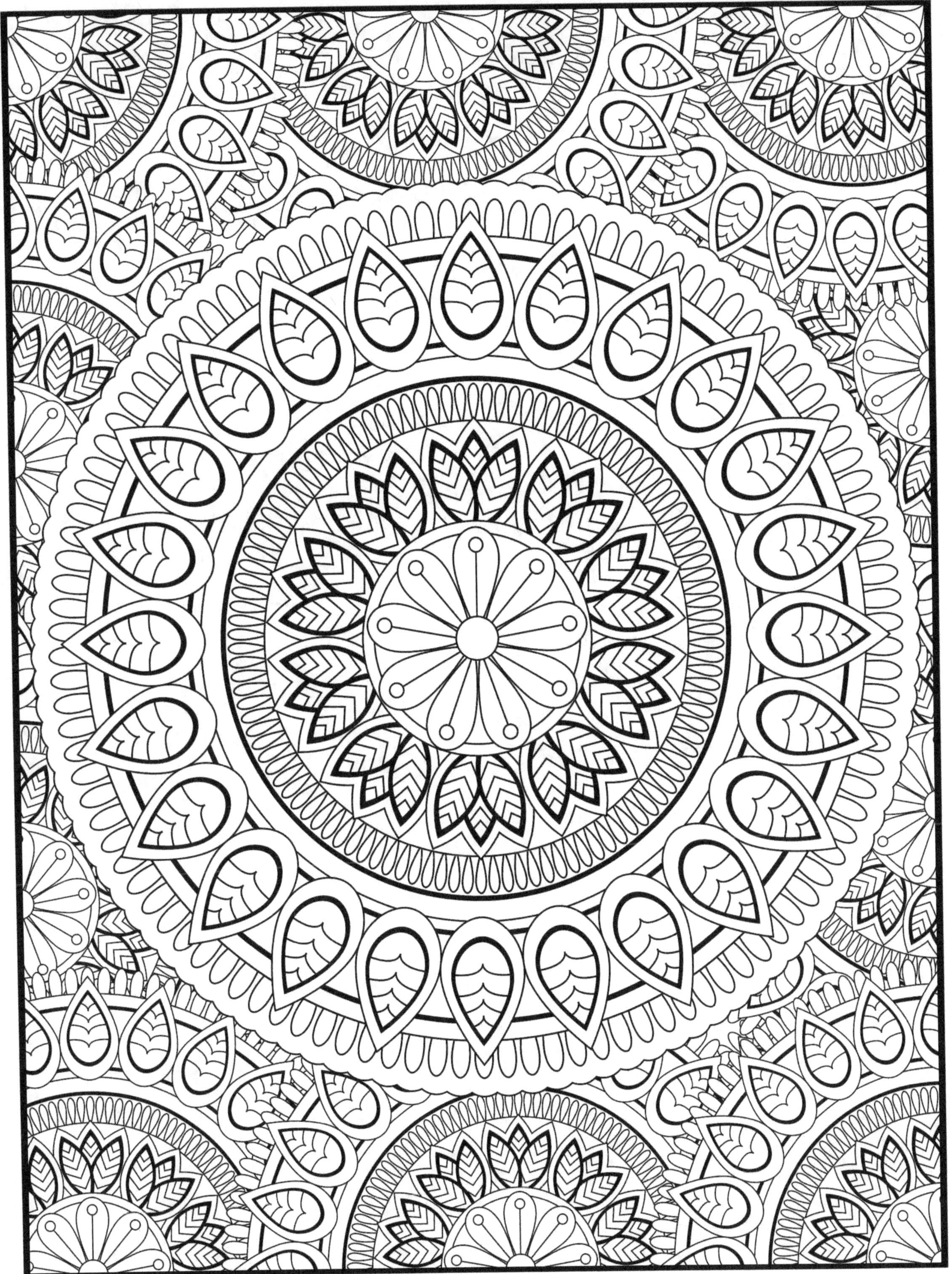

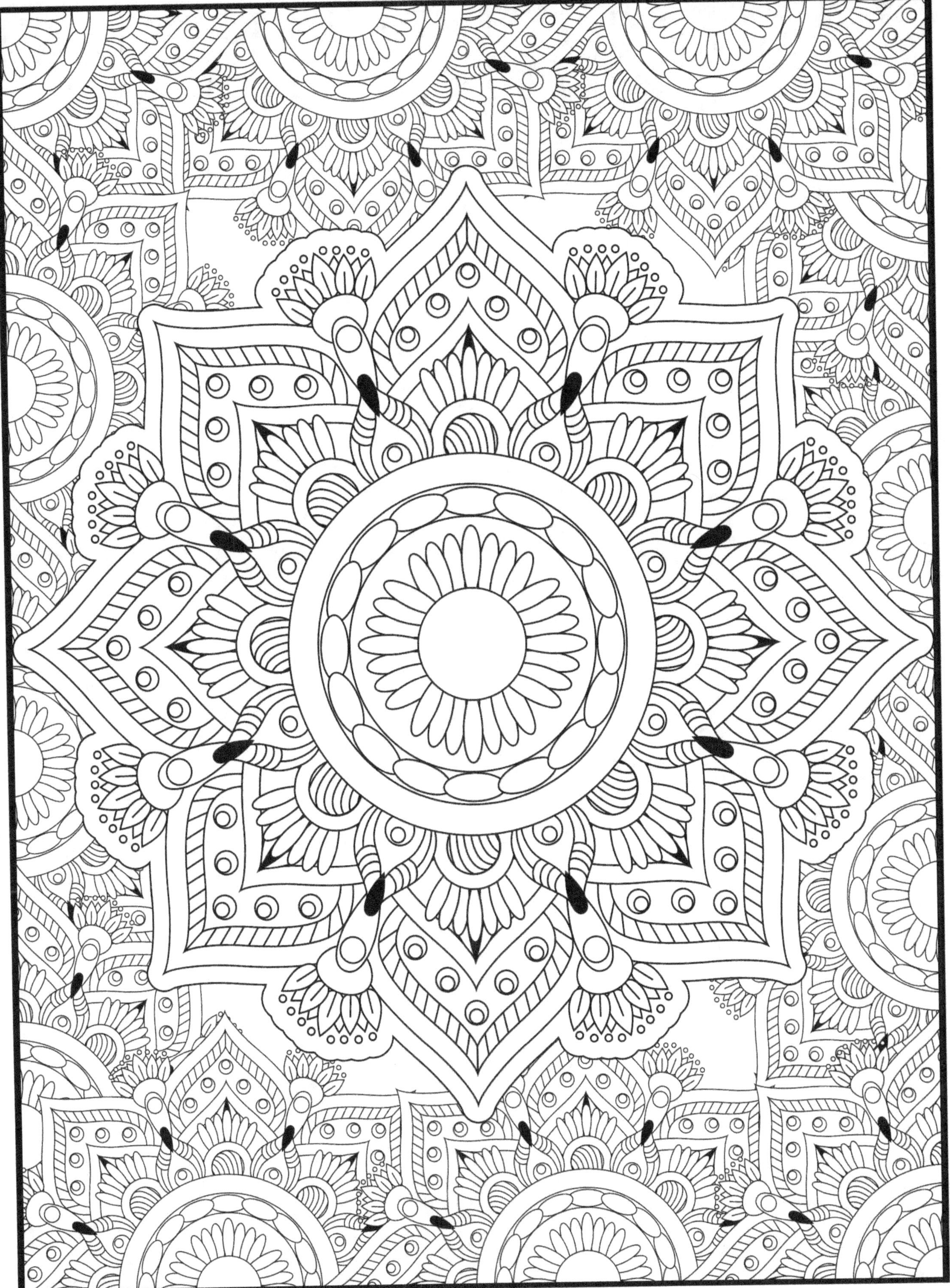

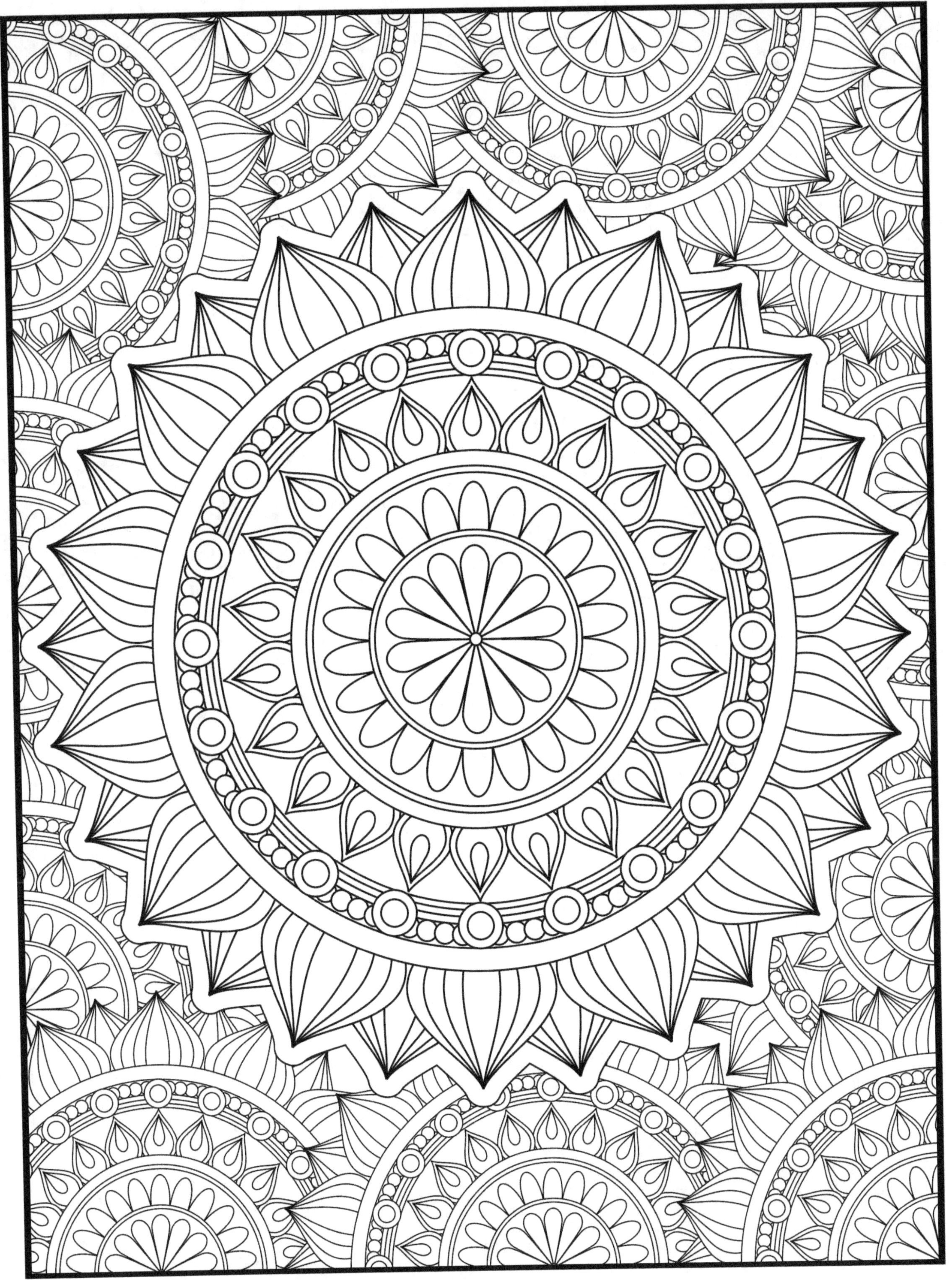

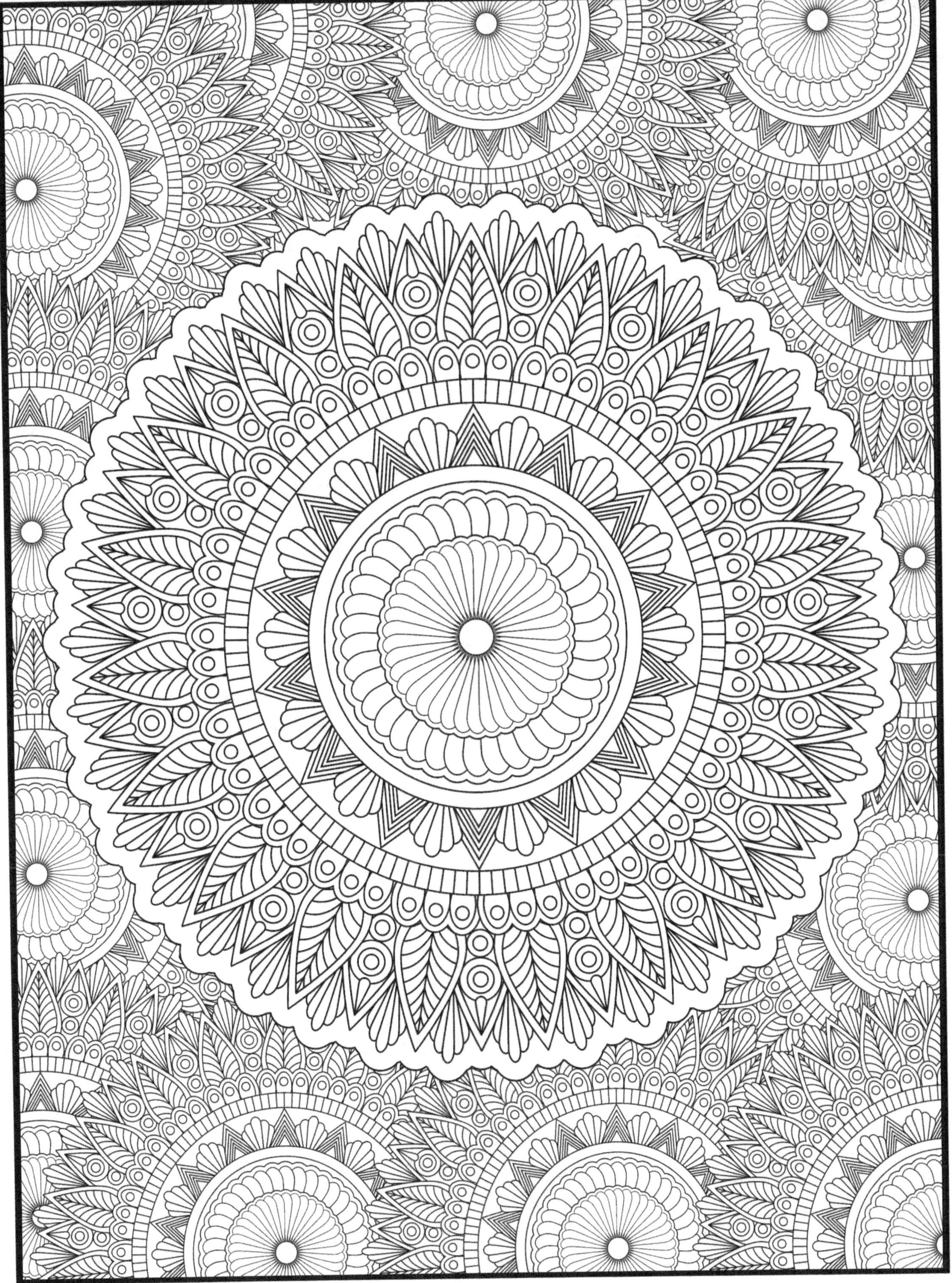

VISIT OUR PUBLICATION SITE FOR OTHER BOOKS

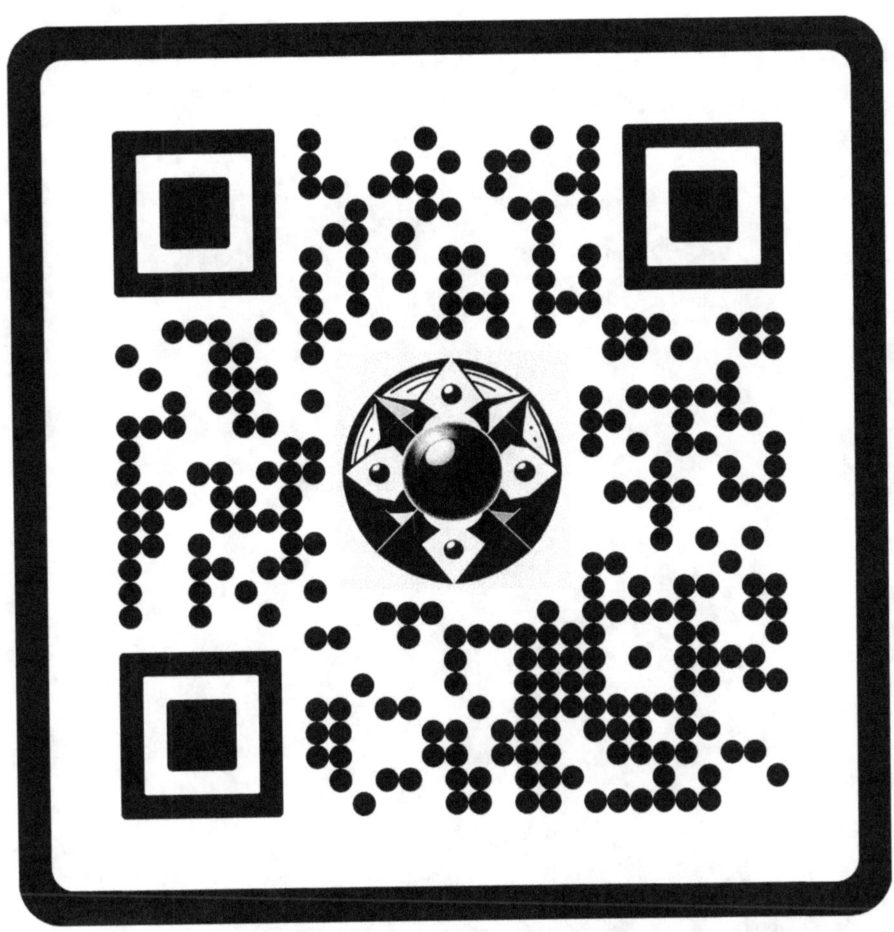

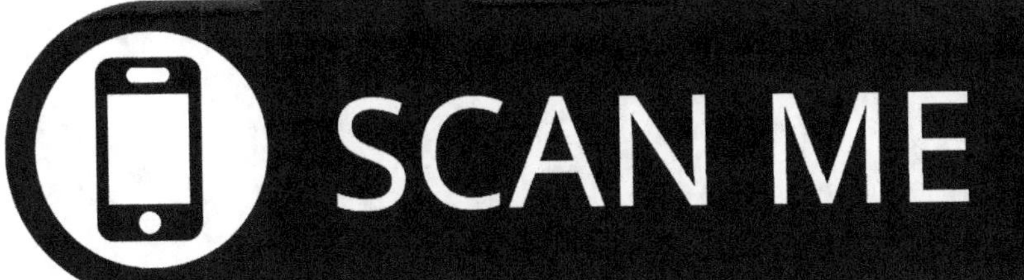

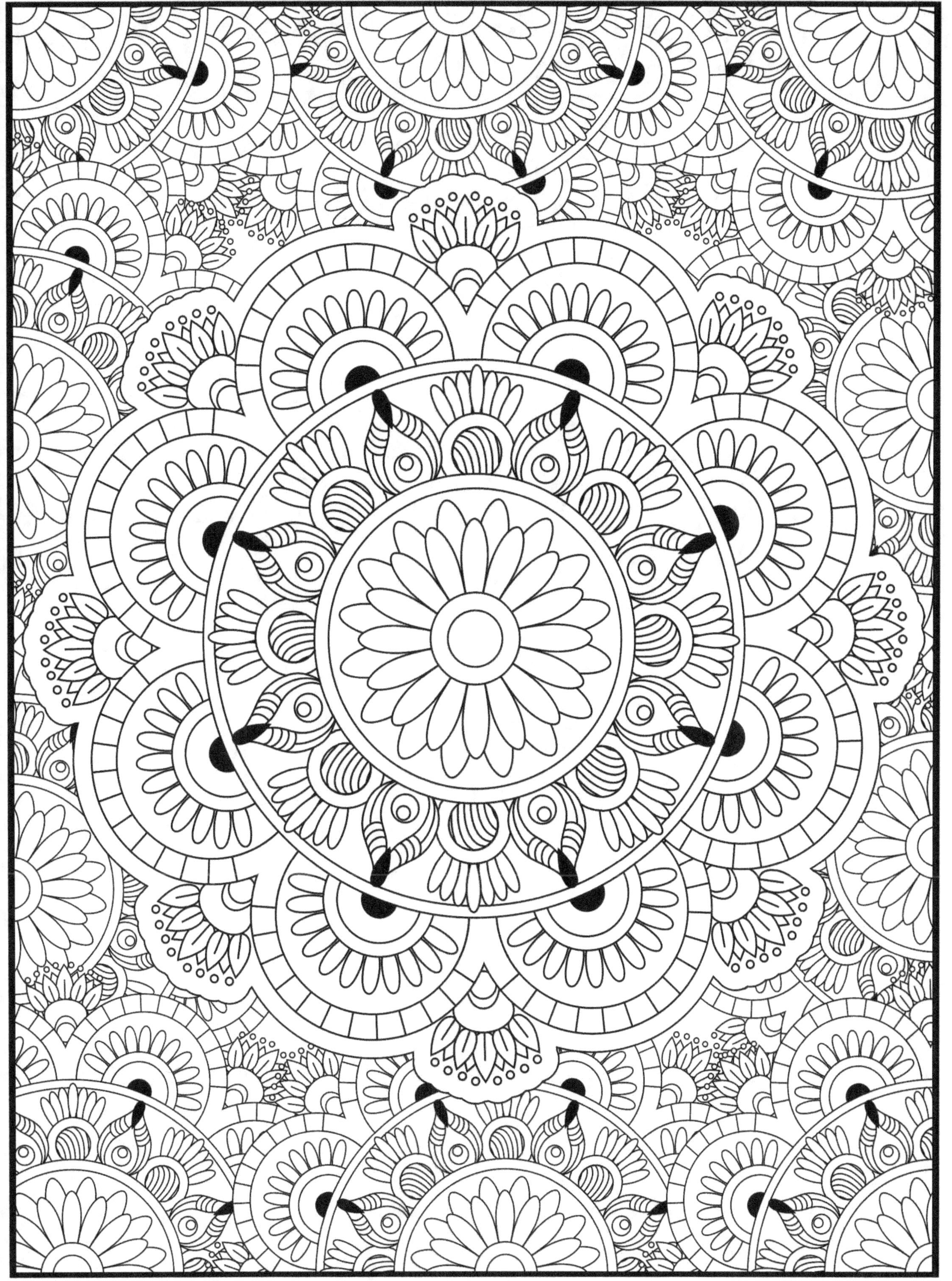